D1603001

Inside the
TOEIC® Exam

Inside the

TOEIC® Exam

Second Edition

By Donald Van Metre
and the Staff of Kaplan Test Prep and Admissions

KAPLAN

PUBLISHING

New York

© 2008 by Kaplan, Inc.

Published by Kaplan Publishing, a division of Kaplan, Inc.
1 Liberty Plaza, 24th Floor
New York, NY 10006

Printed in the United States of America

October 2008
10 9 8 7 6 5 4 3 2 1

ISBN 13: 978-1-4277-9781-0

Kaplan Publishing books are available at special quantity discounts to use for sales promotions, employee premiums, or educational purposes. Please email our Special Sales Department to order or for more information at kaplanpublishing@kaplan.com, or write to Kaplan Publishing, 1 Liberty Plaza, 24th Floor, New York, NY 10006.

Contents

KAPLAN

How to Use This Book

This book provides an overview of the Test of English for International Communication (TOEIC) exam, which has recently been revised. The book includes a content review of the topics that appear on the exam, as well as general tips and strategies designed to help you improve your score.

OVERVIEW OF THE TOEIC EXAM

For an overview of the content and structure of the TOEIC exam, Chapter 1 will be the most useful. It provides:

- General information about the format and structure
- Information about the Secure and Institutional Programs
- An overview of the differences between the old TOEIC exam and the recently revised TOEIC exam
- Information about how the exam is scored

TEST-TAKING TIPS AND STRATEGIES

For general test-taking tips and strategies, Chapter 2 will be the most useful. It provides:

- Key strategies for taking multiple-choice tests

For tips and strategies designed specifically for the TOEIC exam, Chapters 3 and 4 will be the most useful. They provide:

- Tips and Strategies for the Listening and Reading Sections
- Examples, exercises, and explanations for each part of these sections

Good luck on the exam!

Chapter 1:
What's Inside the TOEIC Exam

TOEIC is an acronym for Test of English for International Communication. It is developed and scored by Educational Testing Services (ETS), a nonprofit organization whose mission is to provide testing and assessment services to colleges, universities, and businesses. (For more information about ETS, please visit: *www.ets.org*). The test was first introduced in Japan in 1979 and is now used around the world; it is taken by nearly 5 million people annually.

This multiple-choice test is designed to assess the proficiency of nonnative speakers in general English as it is used in business and the workplace. It does not test *specialized* knowledge of business or workplace English, but rather, it tests everyday English that is used in business environments as well as everyday life.

This pencil and paper test has 200 questions and takes approximately 2½ hours to complete. It is divided into two 100-question sections—*listening* and *reading*—that are timed separately and use photographs, audio, and written texts.

WHO USES THE TOEIC EXAM?

The TOEIC exam is used primarily by businesses. Increasingly, it is being used by colleges, universities, and other academic institutions, and by governments.

In business and government, the test scores are typically used by human resource managers and other decision-makers to help make personnel decisions that affect the hiring, training, promoting, and placement of employees.

In academic settings, the test scores are typically used by admissions offices to help decide whether applicants should be admitted and to identify those individuals who may need to take additional English courses. Language institutes often use the test scores to determine level placement and to assess the progress of students.

SECURE PROGRAM VERSUS INSTITUTIONAL PROGRAM

The test is administered through two programs: the Secure Program (SP) and the Institutional Program (IP).

Secure Program (SP)

The SP (or Open Public Session) is open to the general public and is administered according to a schedule set by ETS. This schedule varies by country. For information on SP scheduling, contact the TOEIC exam representative in your country.

SP exams are new versions of the TOEIC exam that have never been used before. There is usually one SP administration each month, for a total of 12 administrations per year. The SP exams are given at special centers under strict conditions. You must have a TOEIC exam registration card and photo ID to enter the testing site.

All scoring is done by ETS. Score reports for the SP are sent directly to you, the test-taker, and are valid for two years. ETS keeps test scores on file for two years.

Institutional Program (IP)

The IP exams are versions of the test that have been used in previous SP administrations. These exams are administered at the request of a business, academic institution, or government agency and are usually taken on-site at that business's or institution's location. Registration is handled by the client. The IP administration is supervised by both the client's representatives and by ETS staff, but scoring is done by ETS alone.

Score reports for the IP are sent directly to the client (the requesting business or organization). Because that is the case, if you move to another business, academic institution, or government agency, you may be required to retake the exam. Test scores obtained from an IP administration for a particular client are generally not available for use by the test-taker to present to other organizations.

HOW TO REGISTER

For more information on registering for the SP exam, please visit *www.ets.org/toeic*.

HOW THE TOEIC EXAM IS STRUCTURED

The TOEIC exam is divided into two sections: Listening and Reading. Each section is divided into parts. Each part has its own directions.

TOEIC Exam	
Listening Section—100 Questions **4 Parts**	**Reading Section—100 Questions** **3 Parts**
Part 1: Photographs 10 Questions	Part 5: Incomplete Sentences 40 Questions
Part 2: Question–Response 30 Questions	Part 6: Text Completion 12 Questions
Part 3: Short Conversations 30 Questions	Part 7: Reading Comprehension 48 Questions • *Single Reading Passages (28 Single Passage Questions)*
Part 4: Short Talks 30 Questions	• *4 sets of Double Reading Passages (20 Double Passage Questions)*
SECTION TIME 45 minutes	SECTION TIME 75 Minutes
SECTION SCORE 5–495	SECTION SCORE 5–495
TOTAL TIME (LISTENING AND READING) 2.5 Hours *(including time to fill out forms)*	
TOTAL SCORE (LISTENING AND READING) 10–990	

LISTENING SECTION

The Listening Section has four parts. This section takes approximately 45 minutes to complete.

Part 1: Photographs (10 Questions)

In Part 1, you will see a series of 10 photographs. Each photograph is followed by 4 spoken statements. You must pick the statement that best describes what you see in the photograph. The statements are spoken only 1 time, and they are *not* printed in the test book.

The photographs typically show ordinary activities taking place in familiar surroundings, such as a man sitting on a park bench or people having a meeting in an office.

Part 2: Question—Response (30 Questions)

Part 2 consists of a series of 30 questions and statements, each followed by 3 spoken responses. You must pick the response that best answers the question or statement you have heard. The responses are spoken only 1 time, and they are *not* printed in the test book.

The questions and statements typically deal with routine workplace situations or everyday activities.

Part 3: Short Conversations (30 Questions)

Part 3 consists of a series of 10 short conversations each followed by 3 questions. Each question has 4 answer choices. The questions are printed in the test book, and they are narrated 1 time each. The answer choices are printed in the test book *only*. For each question, you must select the best answer choice.

The questions typically ask about the general nature of the conversation, such as where it takes place or who the speakers are, as well as specific details about what was said. The questions generally ask for information in the order that the information is presented in the conversation.

Part 4: Short Talks (30 Questions)

Part 4 consists of a series of 10 short talks each followed by 3 questions. Each question has 4 answer choices. The questions are printed in the test book, and they are narrated 1 time each. The answer choices are printed in the test book *only*. For each question, you must select the best answer choice.

The questions typically ask about the general nature of the talk, such as where it takes place or who the speaker is, as well as specific details about what was said. The questions generally ask for information in the order in which the information is presented in the talk.

READING SECTION

The Reading Section has three parts. This section takes approximately 75 minutes to complete.

Part 5: Incomplete Sentences (40 Questions)

The first part consists of 40 fill-in-the-blanks sentences, each followed by 4 answer choices. For each sentence, you must select the answer choice that best fits in the blank. The sentences can test either vocabulary or grammar.

As soon as you have finished Part 5, you may go on to Part 6.

Part 6: Text Completion (12 Questions)

Part 6 consists of 3 sets of short reading passages. Each passage has 4 fill-in-the-blank sentences, each followed by 4 answer choices. For each sentence, you must select the answer choice that best fits in the blank. The sentences can test either vocabulary or grammar. Some of the words being tested may refer to information contained in either earlier or later sentences in the passage.

As soon as you have finished Part 6, you may go on to Part 7.

Part 7: Reading Comprehension (48 Questions)

Part 7 has two types of reading passages: Single Passages (28 questions) and Double Passages (20 questions).

The *single passages* come first. Each single reading passage is followed by between 2 and 5 questions. Each question has 4 answer choices. For each question, you must select the best answer.

The questions typically ask about details provided in the passage; inferences that can be made based on the information presented; and about the meaning of vocabulary words as they are used in the passage. The questions generally ask about information in the order that the information is presented in the passage.

The *double passages* follow the single passages. There are 4 sets of double reading passages. Each set consists of a pair of passages followed by 5 questions. Each question has 4 answer choices. For each question, you must select the best answer.

Like the questions for the single reading passages, the questions for the double reading passages typically ask about details provided in the passages; inferences that can be made based on the information presented; and the meaning of vocabulary words as they are used in the passages. There is usually at least 1 question that will require you to use information found in both passages. The questions generally ask about information in the order that the information is presented in the passages.

HOW THE EXAM IS SCORED

You will mark your answers on an answer sheet with a pencil. Your answer sheet will be scanned by a computer, and the number of questions (for each section) answered correctly will be converted to a scale that ranges from 5 to 495 for each section.

Only questions you have answered correctly will contribute to your score. You will not be penalized for questions answered incorrectly. Scores are reported separately for each section—Listening and Reading—and also as a total score. The total score is simply the scores for the 2 sections added together: the total score ranges from 10 to 990.

TESTING SCHEDULE

The Secure Program (Open Public Session) is generally administered 12 times a year. The actual number of tests and the test administration dates vary from country to country and from year to year. For up-to-date information about test schedules and registration, please contact your local TOEIC exam administration office.

The IP is administered only by request. If an employer or other organization needs you to take an IP version of the test, it will provide you with details regarding the schedule and registration.

Chapter 2:
Nine Key Strategies for Taking Multiple-Choice Tests

STRATEGY 1: KNOW THE DIRECTIONS IN ADVANCE OF TEST DAY

Each part of the test has its own directions. Knowing what they are *before* you take the test will help you manage your time—you will not have to waste valuable test time listening to or reading the directions if you already know what they are.

In the Listening Section, you will hear the directions for each part before the actual questions begin. (The directions will also be printed in your test book.) While the directions are playing, you should look ahead at the questions that you will be asked to answer. Knowing what the questions are in advance will help you focus on what to listen for.

In the Reading Section, the directions are printed at the beginning of each part. Again, by knowing what the directions are in advance, you will be able to begin answering the questions immediately instead of wasting time reading the directions.

STRATEGY 2: READ EACH QUESTION CAREFULLY BEFORE YOU LOOK AT THE ANSWER CHOICES

Before looking at the answer choices, read the question closely to know what you are being asked. Often, incorrect answer choices are designed to trap you if you misread the question. If you do not understand a question, re-read it slowly. On the exam, the language of the questions and answers is designed to be easier than the language of the material being tested. For example, if you understood the passage (conversation, short talk, reading passage) but do not understand the question, you probably need to re-read the question.

STRATEGY 3: PREDICT THE ANSWER BEFORE LOOKING AT THE CHOICES

After you are clear on what you are required to do, try to predict the answer in your own words—*before looking at the answer choices.*

The questions on the exam are very straightforward—there are no "trick questions" or any questions that require you to calculate or come to a logical conclusion. Information is provided in the listening and reading materials, and the questions try to determine whether you understood that information. If you understand the question, you should be able to answer the question in your own words. Your predicted answer should be among the answer choices.

STRATEGY 4: EVALUATE ALL THE ANSWER CHOICES AND MARK THE ANSWER IF YOU KNOW IT

After you have predicted the answer in your own words, check to see if your answer is among the choices. If the options do not

3 1833 05614 3123

match your predicted answer exactly, choose the option that best matches. Re-read the question to make sure it's a good match and mark your answer on the answer sheet.

STRATEGY 5: ELIMINATE WRONG ANSWER CHOICES AND SELECT THE BEST ANSWER FROM WHAT REMAINS

If the answer you have predicted is *not* among the answer choices, eliminate any answer choices that you know are wrong and choose the best answer from the remaining choices.

If you can eliminate even one wrong option, you will increase your chances of guessing the correct answer. When there are 4 answer choices, you have a 1-in-4 chance of guessing the correct answer. By eliminating 1 choice, you have improved your chances to 1 in 3. If you can eliminate 2 wrong choices, your chances are even better.

STRATEGY 6: ANSWER EASY QUESTIONS BEFORE HARD ONES

The Listening section of the exam is controlled by the recording. You will not be able to skip ahead, nor can you go back to review your answers. You must answer the questions in the Listening section in the order they are presented. In the Reading section, however, you may answer the questions in any order you like.

Generally speaking, the Reading Section is organized from easy to hard: Part 5 is the easiest, Part 6 is more difficult, and Part 7 is the most difficult. Within each part, the questions are generally ordered from easy to hard. The easiest items appear in the beginning, and the most difficult items appear at the end. For this reason, it is best to work through the Reading Section in the order it is presented in the test book.

As you work through the Reading Section, do not spend too much time on any one question. Each question is worth the same number of points. If you spend a lot of time on one question, you will be wasting time you could spend to answer other questions. If you are having trouble answering a question, either guess at the answer or circle the question number on your answer sheet so you can return to it later if there is time. When you have finished all the easy questions, go back and tackle the harder ones that you skipped earlier.

In Part 7 of the Reading Section, the reading passages have between 2 and 5 questions each. Generally, passages with fewer questions are shorter and easier than passages with more questions. Tackle the short passages first.

The passages are usually grouped by the number of questions; usually the passages with 2 questions come before the passages with 3 questions, which come before the passages with 4 questions, and so on. However, this is not always the case. Try to answer all the 2-question passages first, then the 3-question passages, then the 4-question passages, and so on.

For some of the reading passages, there will be a question that asks about how a particular word is used in the passage. These are generally easy questions, and you should try to answer these first. If you are running out of time, look for these questions, find the word in the passage, and try to answer the question. Often, if you know the word being tested, you can eliminate one or two answer choices without even reading the passage.

STRATEGY 7: ANSWER EVERY QUESTION; CHOOSE ONE LETTER TO USE FOR ALL "WILD GUESSES"

Do not leave any questions unanswered. There is no scoring penalty for an incorrect answer on the exam. Your score is the total of all questions answered *correctly*.

If you really do not know the answer to a question, guess. Choose one letter (A, B, C, or D) to use as a "guessing letter." Using the same letter for every guessed question insures that, on average, 25 percent of your guesses will be correct. The TOEIC exam is designed so that in each part, the number of times each letter is correct is about equal. This means there are approximately the same numbers of As, Bs, Cs, and Ds in each part. For example, if you choose D to guess 10 questions in Part 7, you should expect at least 2 or 3 of your guesses to be correct. However, if you guess randomly—picking a different letter for every question—you might not get *any* correct!

STRATEGY 8: WATCH THE CLOCK

The TOEIC exam is a timed test; you are given 45 minutes to complete the Listening Section, and 75 minutes to complete the Reading Section.

For the Listening Section, the timing is controlled by the recording. After each question there will be a pause of between 5 and 8 seconds, during which you must choose and mark your answer (5 seconds for Part 1, and 8 seconds for Parts 2–4). After the pause, the next question, conversation, or passage will begin. You must work quickly so that you do not fall behind the recording.

For the Reading Section, you are given 75 minutes to finish, and you must work at your own pace. Be sure to watch the clock so you know how much time you have left. Work as quickly as you can but avoid making careless mistakes by working too fast.

STRATEGY 9: CHECK YOUR ANSWER SHEET FOR MISTAKES OR UNANSWERED QUESTIONS BEFORE TURNING IT IN

If you finish the test before time is called, check your answer sheet to make sure you have filled in each oval completely and that there are no extra marks on your sheet. Be sure you have filled in only 1 answer for each question. Be sure you have answered every question and that there are no unanswered questions.

If time is running out and you will not be able to finish the test, pick one letter (A, B, C, or D) and fill in the remaining questions on your answer sheet. It is much better to guess at the remaining questions than to leave them unanswered. Your guesses might be correct, which would earn you score points.

Chapter 3:
Strategies for the TOEIC®
Exam Listening Section

The Listening Section of the TOEIC exam has four parts:

Part 1: Photographs

Part 2: Question/Response

Part 3: Conversations

Part 4: Short Talks

Each part has its own directions and strategies and will be discussed separately on the following pages.

Part 1: Photographs

On the first part of the TOEIC, you will see a series of 10 black-and-white photographs in your test book. You will hear 4 statements for each photograph. You must select the statement that best describes what you see in the photograph. The statements are *not* printed in your test book – they are spoken only once, so you must listen carefully.

STRATEGY 1: KNOW THE DIRECTIONS

It is important to understand what you are being asked to do before you take the test. The directions for Part 1 will look like this:

LISTENING TEST

In the Listening Section, you will have the chance to demonstrate how well you understand spoken English. The Listening Section will take approximately 45 minutes. There are four parts, and directions are given for each part. You must mark your answers on the separate answer sheet. Do not write them in the test book.

Part 1

Directions: For each question, you will hear four statements about the picture in your test book. When you hear the statements, choose the one statement that best describes what you see in the picture. Then, find the number of the question on your answer sheet and mark your answer. The statements will not be written in your test book and will be spoken just once.

For the example photograph above, you will hear:

Narrator: *A.*

Woman: *They're leaving the office.*

Narrator: *B.*

Woman: *They're turning off the machine.*

Narrator: *C.*

Woman: *They're gathered around the table.*

Narrator: *D.*

Woman: *They're eating at a restaurant.*

STRATEGY 2: LOOK AT THE FIRST FEW PHOTOGRAPHS WHILE THE DIRECTIONS ARE PLAYING

Knowing the directions in advance gives you an advantage. Because you already know what you will have to do, you should look at the first few photographs in your test book while the directions are playing. This will let you know what to expect, and what you will need to listen for.

As you look at the photographs, think about what they are showing and how that might be described in English.

STRATEGY 3: FOCUS ON THE MAIN ACTION IN THE PHOTOGRAPH AND IDENTIFY IN YOUR OWN WORDS WHAT THE PHOTOGRAPH IS SHOWING

As you look at each photograph, decide what the main action or idea is. The correct statement about the photograph will almost always deal with the most important element in the photograph.

The correct answer will not usually be a minor detail; it will be the answer to this question: *"What is this a picture of?"*

In the sample photograph above, for example, one man is holding a cup of coffee. Educational Testing Services (ETS) would not make the correct answer, *"The man is holding a cup of coffee."* While this statement is true, it is not the main action or element shown in the picture. Ask yourself, *"What is this a picture of?"* Is it a picture of a man holding a cup of coffee? No, it is a picture of three people gathered around a table.

When there are people in the pictures, it can be easy to decide what the main action is. The people are usually doing something. The correct statement will probably be about whatever it is they are doing. But some photographs on the test do not have any people in them; they might show a group of objects or a landscape, for example. With these photographs, it can be more difficult to determine what is being shown.

To help focus on the main action or element in a photograph without people in it, ask yourself:

"Where was this picture taken?"

- If the location is very obvious, such as beach or a parking lot, the answer may be about where the photo was taken.

"What objects are being shown?"

- The answer may be testing whether you know what they are called.

"How are the objects located or positioned?"

- If the photograph shows several objects, the answer may involve the location or position of the objects; for example, whether one object is in front of, on top of, or behind another.

Look at each photograph quickly and decide in your own words what it shows. Each photograph shows one main action or idea; the answer for each photograph (the statement that best describes what is happening) almost always refers to the most obvious action or object in the picture.

As you look at each picture, ask yourself, "*What is this a picture of?*" The answer, in your own words, will usually be very close to what the correct answer will be—except, of course, that it will be in English.

This process is very similar to what ETS does when it chooses the pictures to use for the test. ETS staff look at the photographs and ask themselves, "*What is this a picture of?*" The most common answer becomes the correct statement.

Look again at the example photograph in the directions. What is it a picture of? Your answer is probably something very close to this: "*The people are around a table.*" The correct statement is: "*They're gathered around the table.*"

Most of the time, your first answer to the question "*What is this a picture of?*" will be the correct answer.

STRATEGY 4: EVALUATE THE STATEMENTS YOU HEAR AND MARK THE ANSWER IF YOU KNOW IT.

Once you know in your own words what the picture is showing and have decided on the main action, you must listen to and evaluate the statements you hear. Because each statement will be spoken only once, you must listen carefully.

Listen for a statement that is a close match to what you chose as your answer to the question, "*What is this a picture of?*"

Be sure to listen to all 4 statements before you mark you answer sheet.

If one of the statements is a close match to the answer you have been expecting, find the number for the question on your answer sheet and mark the oval for the letter that matches your answer. Be sure to fill in your oval completely.

STRATEGY 5: ELIMINATE STATEMENTS THAT ARE FALSE AND SELECT THE BEST MATCH FROM WHAT IS LEFT

What if none of the statements match your expected answer very well? You must eliminate any choices that are false. The best way to do that is to repeat each statement to yourself and ask, *"Is this true?"*

Look at directions example again.

Statement (A) *They're leaving the office.* Is this true?

No, it is clearly false. The people are not leaving the office. *Eliminate this choice.*

Statement (B) *They're turning off the machine.* Is this true?

No, this is also false. There is no machine on the table, or anywhere in the room. *Eliminate this choice.*

Statement (C) *They're gathered around the table.* Is this true?

Yes. They are around the table. *Keep this choice.*

Statement (D) *They're eating at a restaurant.* Is this true?

No, this is false. While they are at a table, they are clearly not eating in a restaurant. *Eliminate this choice.*

In this example, only Statement (C) is true: *They're gathered around the table.* Choices (A), (B), and (D) can be eliminated because they are false.

In the directions example, the main action was very clear, and it was easy to identify the statements that were false. What if only one or two choices seem false to you? What if you cannot eliminate all the wrong answers? Then you must select the best match from what is left.

You have already decided what the answer should be in your own words. Do any of the answer choices contain words that are similar to what you expect the correct answer to use? In the directions example, you might expect the words *"around"* or *"table."* The option that contains these words is (C), which is the correct answer.

If you are unable to eliminate answer choices, choose the option that uses words or phrases that are similar to your expected answer.

STRATEGY 6: ANSWER THE CURRENT QUESTION BEFORE THE NEXT SET OF STATEMENTS BEGINS

Answer every question as quickly as you can. You have only about 8 seconds to choose your answer for each photograph. You should be finished with the current question before the next set of statements begins. If you are still answering a question when the next one begins, you might not hear the first statement.

As soon as you have finished with a question, look ahead to the next photograph and ask yourself, *"What is this a picture of?"* Answer in your own words and listen for the statement that most closely matches yours.

STRATEGY 7: KNOW COMMON DISTRACTOR TYPES

There are several kinds of distractors used in Part 1. The most common are:

1. **Wrong word usage**

   This type of distractor asks you to identify the correct vocabulary word or the correct form of a word.

2. **Similar-sounding words**

   This type of distractor sounds similar to the correct answer but the distractors will have different meanings.

3. **Reasonable statements/assumptions**

   This type of distractor may refer to objects or actions in the picture and, therefore, may seem reasonable, but they do not correctly describe what you see. They may also make assumptions about what may (or may not) be happening in the picture.

4. **Irrelevant statements**

   This type of distractor does not describe anything in the picture. Irrelevant statements often use words or phrases that may seem like they should go with the objects or main action in the picture.

5. **Hybrid distractors**

   This type of distractor is a combination of the four types listed above. They combine similar-sounding words, references to objects that may be seen in the picture, or words and phrases that seem like they should go with the objects or main action in the picture.

More than one type of distractor may be used in a picture. Not all distractors fit neatly into these categories; some may seem to belong to more than one category. Note also that each of these distractor types is similar because, in the end, they are false and do not describe what is happening in the picture. However, it is useful to look at *why* they are false and to understand what it is you must listen for.

Each of the common distractor types is discussed separately on the following pages.

Wrong Word Usage

This type of distractor essentially asks you to identify the correct vocabulary word, or the correct form of a word. Each of the choices might, for example, use the same form of a verb but change the nouns they refer to. Or, they might use the correct noun throughout, but change the verbs. Prepositions can also be tested this way. This distractor type is often easy to eliminate.

Example 1

You will hear:

Narrator: *Look at the picture marked number 1 in your test book.*

Narrator: *A.*

Woman: *They're examining the documents.*

Narrator: *B.*

Woman: *They're copying the documents.*

Narrator: *C.*

Woman: *They're writing on the documents.*

Narrator: *D.*

Woman: *They're e-mailing the documents.*

The correct statement is Choice (A) *They're examining the documents.*

Choices (B), (C), and (D) all use the wrong verb to describe what is happening. This is essentially a vocabulary item.

Similar-Sounding Words

This type of distractor uses words that sound similar to the correct answer.

Example 2

You will hear:

Narrator: *Look at the picture marked number 2 in your test book.*

Narrator: *A.*

Woman: *The man is changing his tie.*

Narrator: *B.*

Woman: *The man is putting out a fire.*

Narrator: *C.*

Woman: *The man is changing a tire.*

Narrator: *D.*

Woman: *The man is going to retire.*

The correct statement is Choice (C) *The man is changing a tire.* Choices (A), (B), and (D) all use words that sound similar to *tire* (e.g., *tie, fire, retire*).

Sometimes the similar-sounding words will be nouns (as in choices (A) and (B) above). At other times, the similar-sounding words may be verbs (as in choice (D) above) or other parts of speech.

Reasonable Statements/Assumptions

This type of distractor may refer to objects or actions in the picture and, therefore, may seem reasonable, but the statement does not correctly describe what you see. It may also make assumptions about what may (or may not) be happening in the picture. When a statement makes an assumption, it is usually wrong.

Example 3

You will hear:

Narrator: *Look at the picture marked number 3 in your test book.*

Narrator: *A.*

Woman: *The man is working at his desk.*

Narrator: *B.*

Woman: *The man has just sat down in the chair.*

Narrator: *C.*

Woman: *The man is installing software on his computer.*

Narrator: *D.*

Woman: *The man is deleting e-mail.*

The correct statement is Choice (A) *The man is working at his desk.*

Choice (B) uses the words *sat down* and *chair* because the man is, in fact, sitting in a chair; however, we do not know whether or not he has *just sat down*—meaning he sat down very recently. He may have been sitting there for several hours. This is an example of a reasonable statement that also makes an assumption.

Choice (C) uses the word *computer* because we can see a computer in the picture; however, we do not know whether or not the man is *installing software.* Again, this is an example of a reasonable statement that also makes an assumption.

Choice (D) uses the phrase *deleting e-mail,* because that is an activity that can be associated with using a computer; however, we do not know whether or not he is deleting e-mail, writing e-mail, opening a document, or performing some other activity. This is another example of a reasonable statement that also makes an assumption.

Irrelevant Statements

This type of distractor uses statements that do not describe anything in the picture. It often uses words or phrases that may seem like they should go with the objects or main action in the picture.

Example 4

You will hear:

Narrator: *Look at the picture marked number 4 in your test book.*

Narrator: *A.*

Man: *The waiter is setting the table.*

Narrator: *B.*

Man: *The spoons are next to the forks.*

Narrator: *C.*

Man: *The food is in the refrigerator.*

Narrator: *D.*

Man: *The dishes are stacked on shelves.*

The correct statement is Choice (D) *The dishes are stacked on shelves.*

Choice (A) refers to *a waiter* and *setting the table*, which can both be associated with *dishes*; however, this statement does not describe anything that can be seen in the picture.

Choice (B) refers to *spoons* and *forks*, which again are both associated with *dishes*; however, this statement does not describe anything that can be seen in the picture.

Choice (C) refers to *food* and a *refrigerator*, which can both be associated with *dishes*; however, this statement does not describe anything that can be seen in the picture.

Hybrid Distractors

This type of distractor combines similar sounding words, references to objects that may be seen in the picture, or words and phrases that seem like they should go with the objects or main action in the picture. These distractors are working to distract you on several levels at once. They are very common, and they are usually the most difficult to eliminate.

Example 5

You will hear:

Narrator: *Look at the picture marked number 5 in your test book.*

> Narrator: *A.*
>
> Woman: *He's watering the plants.*
>
> Narrator: *B.*
>
> Woman: *He's putting on glasses.*
>
> Narrator: *C.*
>
> Woman: *He's getting some water.*
>
> Narrator: *D.*
>
> Woman: *He's spilling water from a cup.*

The correct statement is Choice (C) *He's getting some water.*

Choice (A) uses the word *watering*, which is similar to the expected word, *water*. It is also an irrelevant statement because there are no *plants* in the picture, and the statement does not describe what is happening. This hybrid distractor is a combination of similar-sounding words and an irrelevant statement.

Choice (B) uses the word *glasses*. We might expect the correct answer to use the word *cup* or *glass*. The word *glasses* sounds similar to the word *glass,* but *glasses* refers in this case to *eyeglasses*. There are no *glasses* in the picture, so the statement does not describe what is happening. This hybrid distractor is a combination of similar-sounding words and an irrelevant statement.

Choice (D) uses the word *spilling*, which sounds similar to the expected word *filling*. It also uses the expected words *water* and *cup*; however, the statement does not describe what is happening. This hybrid distractor is a combination of similar-sounding words and a reasonable statement.

Strategy Summary, Part I

- Know the directions.

- Look ahead at the photographs while the directions are playing.

- Focus on the main action and ask yourself *"What is this a picture of?"*

- Evaluate the answer choices.

- Eliminate as many answer choices as you can.

- Answer each question before the next one starts.

- Understand the common distractor types.

PRACTICE QUESTIONS

Note that during the exam, *you will not be able to read the statements;* they will be narrated, and you will hear them only once.

Following are examples of the kinds of photographs that will appear in the test book, and the statements that you will hear about the photographs. Answers and explanations begin on page 43.

Directions

For each photograph, read the statements and mark the answer
choice that best describes what you see.

Practice 1

(A) The man is cutting some paper.
(B) The man is preparing for a meeting.
(C) The man is sharpening the knife.
(D) The man is carving the meat.

Mark Your Answer:

Practice 2

(A) They're standing around a piano.
(B) They're playing instruments.
(C) They're watching a concert.
(D) They're listening to music.

Mark Your Answer:

Practice 3

(A) Cars are parked along the highway.
(B) A truck is being filled with fuel.
(C) Cars are being repaired.
(D) A truck is turning at the corner.

Mark Your Answer:

Practice 4

(A) The man is reaching for a book.
(B) The man is setting down a chair.
(C) The man is reading a magazine.
(D) The man is holding a news conference.

Mark Your Answer:

ANSWERS AND EXPLANATIONS

Practice 1

(A) The man is cutting some paper.

(B) The man is preparing for a meeting.

(C) The man is sharpening the knife.

(D) The man is carving the meat.

Explanation: Ask yourself: *What is this a picture of?* **It is a picture of someone cutting some meat. The correct answer is Choice (D).**

Choice (A) uses the word *cutting*, which is an action that can be seen in the picture; however, the man is cutting meat, not paper. This can be seen as either a "reasonable statement" or a "wrong word" distractor—or even as a hybrid of the two.

Choice (B) uses the phrase *preparing for a meeting,* which sounds a little like *preparing meat.* The man is preparing something, but he is not preparing for a meeting. This can be seen as an example of a hybrid "similar sound" and "wrong word" distractor.

Choice (C) refers to a *knife,* which can be seen in the picture; however, the man is not sharpening it. This is an example of a "reasonable statement" distractor.

Practice 2

(A) They're standing around a piano.

(B) They're playing instruments.

(C) They're watching a concert.

(D) They're listening to music.

Explanation: Ask yourself: *What is this a picture of?* It is a picture of three people standing next to a piano. The correct answer is Choice (A).

Choice (B) uses the phrase *playing instruments* because the piano is an instrument that people can play. However, none of the people are playing the piano or any other instruments. This is an example of a "reasonable statement" distractor.

Choice (C) uses the phrase *watching a concert,* which might be associated with the piano visible in the picture. However, this does not describe what is happening. This is an example of an "irrelevant statement" distractor.

Choice (D) uses the phrase *listening to music;* however, it does not appear that anyone is playing the piano. We cannot assume that music is being played somewhere else. This is an example of an "irrelevant statement" distractor.

Practice 3

(A) Cars are parked along the highway.
(B) A truck is being filled with fuel.
(C) Cars are being repaired.
(D) A truck is turning at the corner.

Explanation: Ask yourself: *What is this a picture of?* It is a picture of traffic on a city street. We can see a truck making a turn at the corner. The correct answer is Choice (D).

Choice (A) uses the word *cars*, which we can see in the picture. However, the cars are not parked, and this is not a highway. This is an example of an "irrelevant statement" distractor.

Choice (B) uses the word *truck*, which we can see in the picture. However, the truck is not being filled with fuel. This is an example of an "irrelevant statement" distractor.

Choice (C) uses the word *cars*, which we can see in the picture. However, the cars are not being repaired. This is an example of an "irrelevant statement" distractor.

Practice 4

(A) The man is reaching for a book.
(B) The man is setting down a chair.
(C) The man is reading a magazine.
(D) The man is holding a news conference.

Explanation: Ask yourself: *What is this a picture of?* **This is a picture of a man sitting down reading a magazine. The correct answer is Choice (C).**

Choice (A) uses the word *reaching*, which sounds a little like reading, and it uses the expected word *book*. However, the man is not reaching for anything. The statement does not describe what is happening. This is an example of a "similar sound" distractor; it can also be seen as a "reasonable statement" distractor—or even as a hybrid of the two.

Choice (B) uses the phrase *setting down*, which sounds like the expected phrase *sitting down*. This is an example of a "similar sound" distractor.

Choice (D) uses the word *holding*, because we can see that the man is holding something. It also uses the phrase news conference, which might be confused with newspaper. This statement does not describe what is happening. This is an example of a hybrid "similar sound" and "irrelevant statement" distractor.

Part 2: Question–Response

On the second part of the TOEIC, you will hear a series of 30 questions or statements, each followed by 3 responses. (Most of the items in Part 2 are questions; there are usually only 3 or 4 statements.) You must select the best response to the question or statement. The questions and the responses are *not* printed in your test book—because they are spoken only once, you must listen carefully.

STRATEGY 1: KNOW THE DIRECTIONS

It is important to understand what you are being asked to do *before* you take the test. The directions for Part 2 will look like this:

> **Directions:** You will hear a question or statement and three responses spoken in English. They will be spoken only once and will not be printed in your test book. Choose the best response to the question or statement and mark the letter on your answer sheet.

STRATEGY 2: KNOW THE DIFFERENT QUESTION TYPES

The question types that are found on the TOEIC exam can be divided into 4 broad categories:

1. *Wh-* information
2. Choice
3. Yes/No
4. Tag

Knowing the different kinds of question types will help you to anticipate answers and to eliminate distractors.

Each question type will be discussed in further detail on the following pages.

Wh- Information Questions

Wh- information questions are the most common type of question on the exam. They use question words (*Who, What, Where, Why, When,* and *How*). They ask about details and require answers that provide specific information. The correct answers are usually not simply *Yes* or *No*.

Question Word	Examples
What + verb	
Common verbs for *What* questions are:	
do	What *does* Technoline Inc. charge for its services?
be	What *aren't* we supposed to delete?
have	What *have* you told Sarah regarding the mix-up?
will	What *will* George say about the cost overruns?
can	What *can't* they ship by today?
could	What *could* we do to improve office morale?
should	What *should* have been done differently?
would	What *wouldn't* you want to change in the current contract?
might	What *might* be causing the delay in shipping?
The verbs that follow *What* can occur in all tenses, and they can be positive or negative.	
What + verb questions cover a large number of topics. There is no "formula" for predicting the correct answers. The answers will depend on the specific verbs used in the questions.	

Question Word	Examples
What + noun/noun phrase *What* can be followed by singular or plural nouns or noun phrases. *What + noun/noun phrase* questions cover a large number of topics. There is no "formula" for predicting the correct answers; the answers will depend on the specific nouns or noun phrases used in the questions.	What reason did they give for not paying on time? What time is the meeting? What day would be best for you? What plans do you have for expanding your market share? What kind of company is Troglodyne? What types of products does your company sell? What sort of person would be good at this job?
What idioms Certain idioms or fixed expressions are formed with *What*. *What about* can be used to make a suggestion. The answer will usually be either an agreement or disagreement with the suggestion, plus a reason for agreeing or disagreeing (e.g., *That's a good idea, but . . .*). *What about* can also be used to ask the status of something. *What if* asks about a possibility—a situation that has not happened but that is possible.	What about ... What if ... *What about offering a discount on volume purchases?* [Suggestion] *What about their plan to downsize the workforce?* [Asking about status] What if we hired temporary workers over the holidays? What if nobody likes the new advertisement?

Question Word	Examples
Where + verb	
Common verbs for *Where* questions are:	
do	Where *did* you put the folder for the Johnson project?
be	Where *is* the best place in town to go for sushi?
have	Where *have* you decided to open your next store?
will	Where *will* the new secretary's desk go?
can	Where *can* I find more information about your products and services?
could	Where *could* we go to get a better price?
should	Where *should* I send the invoice?
would	Where *would* you like me to put these boxes?
The verbs that follow *Where* can occur in all tenses, and they can be positive or negative.	
The answer to a *Where* question will be a location, often with a preposition (e.g., *On Smith Street; On my desk; Over there; At the post office; To the warehouse,* etc.).	

Question Word	Examples
Who + verb Common verbs for _Who_ questions are:	
do	Who _didn't_ respond to our questionnaire?
be	_Who's_ in charge of marketing at Brayburn Inc.?
have	Who _has_ the authority to make budget changes?
will	Who _will_ we send to the seminar?
can	Who _can_ we contact to get more information?
could	Who _could_ have known about our plans?
should	Who _should_ we call to get the copier fixed?
would	Who _would_ be the best candidate for further training?
might	Who _might_ be interested in partnering with us on the project?
The verbs that follow _Who_ can occur in all tenses, and they can be positive or negative. The answer to a _Who_ question can be a person's or a company's name (e.g., _John Wilson; Mrs. Smith; Glaxon Industries_), a group (e.g., _Our customers; The board of directors_), or a person's title or rank (e.g., _The accountant, President Kim_).	

Question Word	Examples
Why + verb	
Common verbs for *Why* questions are:	
do	Why *don't* you carry your full line of products at all your stores?
be	Why *were* the paychecks sent out late this week?
have	Why *hasn't* more been done to increase production efficiency?
will	Why *won't* Rebecca be at the meeting?
can	Why *can* Gore Brothers make the same product for less than we can?
could	Why *couldn't* we have gotten a better discount?
should	Why *should* we wait another month?
would	Why *wouldn't* they send the parts right away?
might	Why *might* Tom not like the plan?
The verbs that follow *Why* can occur in all tenses, and they can be positive or negative.	
The answer to a *Why* question will be a reason or explanation. Often, answers will began with *Because* ... or *To* ...	

Question Word	Examples
When + verb Common verbs for *When* questions are:	
do	When *did* they sign the agreement?
be	When *was* Alan supposed to be here?
have	When *has* the meeting been scheduled for?
will	When *will* the next train arrive?
can	When *can* I expect my order to be delivered?
could	When *couldn't* you go?
should	When *should* we leave for the airport?
would	When *would* be a good time to call back?
might	When *might* the layoffs occur?
The verbs that follow *When* can occur in all tenses, and they can be positive or negative; however, negative questions are uncommon. The answer to a *When* question will usually indicate a time (e.g., *On Friday; Tomorrow; At five o'clock; In six months*).	

Question Word	Examples
***How* + verb** Common verbs for *How* questions are: do	 How *did* SymTech get its start?
be	How *were* you planning to advertise the products?
have	How *have* the new tax laws affected us?
will	How *will* we measure the plan's success?
can	How *can* customers contact us?
could	How *could* we better invest our profits?
should	How *should* the president of XgenriX Inc. have responded to the situation?
would	How *would* you improve our website?
might	How *might* we get more data about our customers?
The verbs that follow *How* can occur in all tenses, and they can be positive or negative. The answer to a *How* + *verb* question will indicate the way in which something is done, or it will indicate an action that can or should be taken. Often, the answer will begin with *By* (e.g., *By sending a fax; By filling out a form; By bus*).	

Question Word	Examples
How + adjective	
Common adjectives for *How* questions are:	
many	How *many* employees does your company have?
much	How *much* are these?
large	How *large* is the freight elevator?
big	How *big* is your largest store?
small	How *small* are the rooms?
fast	How *fast* can you get the order out?
slow	How *slow* were they to pay?
different	How *different* are the two plans?
similar	How *similar* were the offers?
long	How *long* will it take to ship?
near	How *near* the airport is the hotel?
far	How *far* is the warehouse from here?
close	How *close* are they to being finished?
The answer to a *How + adjective* question will indicate a degree or an amount (e.g., *Very large; Not far; Ten minutes; Six hours*).	

Question Word	Examples
How + adverb Common adverbs for *How* questions are: often	 How *often* is the website content updated?
quickly	How *quickly* can the project be finished?
swiftly	How *swiftly* can we get it done?
slowly	How *slowly* does the machine need to run?
cheaply	How *cheaply* can we make them?
The answer to a *How + adverb* question will indicate a degree or an amount (e.g., *Fairly often; In two days; For five dollars each*).	

Question Word	Examples
How idioms	
How come ...	How come nobody's ever on time for meetings?
	How come I'm always the one who has to stay late?
	How come the copier's always out of toner?
How is it that ...	How is it that Randy did all the work, but Jared got all the credit?
	How is it that our competitors are doing so well?
	How is it that profits are down when sales are up?
How about ...	How about offering employees more overtime opportunities?
	How about taking a break?
	How about getting John's input on this?
How come ... and _How is it that_ ... can both be used to complain. Answers to these questions will usually be reasons or explanations, often using _Because_ ... or _To_	
How come ... and _How is it that_ ... are both similar to _Why_ questions.	
How about is a suggestion. The answer will usually be either an agreement or disagreement with the suggestion, plus a reason for agreeing or disagreeing (e.g., _That's a good idea, but_ ...).	

Choice Questions

Choice questions ask about choices and preferences. They require answers that provide specific information. In this respect, they are actually a type of information question. Choice questions are common on the exam.

Choice questions often use the initial question word *Which*.

Which suit do you like better?

The expected answer should indicate a specific choice or preference:

The blue one.

Often, choice questions present the choices using the word *or:*

Would you like coffee or tea?

The expected answer should indicate a specific choice or preference.

Coffee, please, with a little cream.

Common phrases used in choice questions include:

Which one/ones ...
Which of these/those ...
Which kind of/kinds of ...
Which do you prefer ...
Which do you like better ...
Which would you choose ...
Would you like A or B ...

Common verbs used in choices questions include the following. These all indicate that a choice or preference is being asked about.

like   want

prefer   choose

If you hear a choice question, listen for a response that indicates a preference or choice. The answer to a choice question is usually not simply *Yes* or *No*.

Yes/No Questions

Yes/No questions require an answer that is either *Yes, No,* or an expression of uncertainty, such as, "I don't know" or "I'm not sure."

Are you going to the conference in San Francisco?

This question requires a *yes/no* response—either *Yes, No,* or an expression of uncertainty:

Yes I am.

No I'm not.

I'm not sure.

Of course, other information can be added to the response:

Yes, in fact, I'll be making a presentation.

No, they're sending John instead.

I'm not sure; they might send John.

Note that the *yes/no* can be implied—not stated directly:

> *I'll be making a presentation.*
> *They're sending John instead.*
> *They might send John.*

Some common ways to say or imply "yes" include:

Okay	No problem
Sure	I'd be glad to

Some common ways to say or imply "no" include:

Not really	I'm afraid not
Unfortunately	

Some common ways to say or imply uncertainty include:

I'm not sure	I think so	Maybe
I don't know	I don't think so	

There are many kinds of *Yes/No* questions. Following are the most common kinds that appear on the exam.

Verb	Examples
***Do* + subject pronoun + infinitive** The verb *Do* can occur in the present or past tense, and it can be positive or negative.	Do I need to work this Saturday? Do you go to the gym every day? Doesn't she work in the Accounting Department? Does it require special training to use? Didn't they guarantee payment within 90 days? Didn't we ship their order on Monday?
***Do* + possessive adjective + noun** The verb *Do* can occur in the present or past tense, and it can be positive or negative. The nouns can be singular or plural.	Does my staff need to attend the meeting? Do your records match ours? Does his boss know what he's been doing? Don't its parts need to be serviced soon? Didn't our order get sent out on time? Did their payment clear?

Verb	Examples
Do + -ing The verb *Do* can occur in the present or past tense, and it can be positive or negative.	Does paying in cash mean we'll get a discount? Did hiring more workers help your production problem? Doesn't shipping by air cost more? Didn't installing the wireless network take a lot of time?
Be + subject pronouns + adjectives The verb *Be* can occur in the present or past tense, and it can be positive or negative.	Am I late for the meeting? Are you happy with your new job? Is Mr. Murphy sick today? Is it faster than the old one? Are they expensive? Aren't we lucky to have Phoebe on our staff?
Be + subject pronouns + -ing The verb *Be* can occur in the present or past tense, and it can be positive or negative.	Am I doing this correctly? Are you waiting to speak to Mr. Crawford? Isn't Julie Reiss running the department these days? Is it operating more efficiently since it was upgraded? Are they coming to the party? Weren't we expecting a delivery from QualComp today?

Verb	Examples
Have + subject pronoun + past participle The verb _Have_ can occur in the present or past tense, and it can be positive or negative.	Have I worked here long enough to qualify for benefits? Haven't you finished the Scottsdale report yet? Has she called you about the cost estimate? Hasn't it cost too much money already? Hadn't they asked us to bill their client directly? Haven't we changed vendors?
Can/Could + subject pronoun + infinitive The verbs _Can/Could_ can be positive or negative.	Can I send the documents to your home instead of your office? Could you come to work a little early tomorrow? Couldn't she find a cheaper apartment? Can it go any faster than that? Couldn't they hire you on a tempo-rary basis? Can't we return it if it's damaged?

Verb	Examples
Could + subject pronoun + have + past participle The verb *Could* can be positive or negative.	Couldn't I have gone with him? Could you have finished quicker if you had better tools? Couldn't he have gotten a better price somewhere else? Could it have been due to a clerical error? Couldn't they have waited a little longer? Could we have raised our prices too high?
Will + subject pronoun + infinitive The verb *Will* can be positive or negative.	Won't I need to bring my own tools? Will you take your laptop with you? Will she know where to go when she gets there? Will it work when the temperature is below freezing? Will they have enough time to finish everything? Won't we pay in cash?

Verb	Examples
Will + possessive adjective + noun The verb *Will* can be positive or negative.	Will my paycheck be ready by this afternoon? Will your company be adding any more staff? Will his plan get approval from the board? Won't its sales just continue to decline? Will our software work on their system? Won't their Web site be updated daily?
Will + -ing The verb *Will* can be positive or negative.	Will repairing the computer be cheaper than buying a new one? Won't making reservations online be faster? Will taking this medicine on an empty stomach make me feel nauseated? Won't traveling by yourself be lonely?

Verb	Examples
Would + subject pronoun + infinitive The verb *Would* can be positive or negative.	Would I need to get approval first? Would you buy more if we lowered our price? Would he charge extra for overnight delivery? Would it look better if we painted it blue? Wouldn't they prefer to stay at the Wexler Hotel? Wouldn't we make more money by investing in high-risk bonds?
Would + possessive adjective + noun The verb *Would* can be positive or negative.	Would my salary go up if I take the new position? Would your office be a more convenient place to meet? Would her boss really say something like that? Would its parts break less frequently if they were serviced more often? Would their services be of use to us? Would our staff be willing to work overtime on short notice?

Verb	Examples
Would + -ing The verb *Would* can be positive or negative.	Would working from home be a possibility? Wouldn't buying in bulk quantities be less expensive? Would billing you monthly be more convenient? Wouldn't flying be quicker than driving?
Should + subject pronoun + infinitive The verb *Should* can be positive or negative	Should I arrange a meeting with John? Shouldn't you make your presentation first? Should Lisa call to make the reservations? Shouldn't it be held in the conference room, instead? Should they upgrade their entire manufacturing system? Should we go to a later show?

Verb	Examples
Should + possessive adjective + noun The verb *Should* can be positive or negative.	Should my accountant call you back to discuss the details? Shouldn't your order have been delivered by now? Should his file be updated? Shouldn't its parts be oiled every day? Should their offer be accepted? Shouldn't our department handle matters like that?
Should + -ing The verb *Should* can be positive or negative.	Should smoking be banned in public places? Shouldn't training be required for all new employees? Should billing be quarterly? Shouldn't buying online be cheaper?

Tag Questions

Tag questions come at the end of sentences. They are used to check information, ask for agreement, or find out whether something is true. They are more common in spoken English than they are in written English.

Tag questions are really a kind of *Yes/No* question.

Chris works in the accounting department, doesn't he?

In this case, the question is checking whether or not Chris works in the accounting department. The speaker thinks this might be true but is not sure. Notice that the expected answer is *Yes, No,* or an expression of uncertainty:

No, he works in the marketing department.

Tag questions repeat the auxiliary verb used in the sentence:

David <u>can</u> come on Friday, <u>can't</u> he?

The capital of France <u>is</u> Paris, <u>isn't</u> it?

You <u>don't</u> take the subway to work, <u>do</u> you?

You <u>haven't</u> seen my glasses anywhere, <u>have</u> you?

Notice that the tag is negative when the sentence verb is positive, and it is positive when the sentence verb is negative:

John Mayer <u>is</u> the CEO of Exitron, <u>isn't</u> he?
       [+]   [-]

John Mayer <u>isn't</u> the CEO of Exitron, <u>is</u> he?
            [-]   [+]

If the sentence does not have an auxiliary verb, the question tag always uses a form of *do:*

You <u>remembered</u> to send the invoices, <u>didn't</u> you?

Sarah <u>made</u> the reservations, <u>didn't</u> she?

Mr. Lee <u>likes</u> to play golf, <u>doesn't</u> he?

Mark <u>goes</u> on vacation next week, <u>doesn't</u> he?

STRATEGY 3: UNDERSTAND THE TYPES OF DISTRACTORS

There are 4 basic types of distractors for Part 2 items:

1. **Similar-sounding words**

   This type of distractor uses words and phrases that sound similar to the expected correct response.

2. **Repetition of question words**

   This type of distractor repeats words and phrases used in the question or statement.

3. **Irrelevant responses**

   This type of distractor responds to a common misunderstanding of the question or statement. Also included in this category are *Yes/No* answers to *Wh-information* questions and *Wh-information* answers to *Yes/No* questions.

4. **Hybrid distractors**

   This type of distractor uses combinations of the first 3 distractor types.

Look at the Part 2 directions example again. You will hear:

Man:	*Where are we meeting?*
Narrator:	*A.*
Woman:	*To meet the new supervisor.*
Narrator:	*B.*
Woman:	*It's the second room on the left.*
Narrator:	*C.*
Woman:	*No, at three o'clock.*

Choice (A) uses the word *meet*, which is a repetition of the word *meeting* in the question. This is an example of a "repetition" distractor. Choice (C) does not answer the question; however, if you misunderstood the question as *When is the meeting?*, this would be an appropriate response. This is an example of an "irrelevant response" distractor.

Here is another example. You will hear:

Woman:	*How many cups of coffee do you usually drink each day?*
Narrator:	*A.*
Man:	*No more than two.*
Narrator:	*B.*
Man:	*I have two copies.*
Narrator:	*C.*
Man:	*I think that's too many.*

The correct response is (A): *No more than two.*

Choice (B) uses the word *copies*, which sounds similar to *coffee* or *coffees*. This is an example of a "similar-sound" distractor. (C) repeats the question word *many*, and it uses the word *too*, which sounds like the expected word *two*. This is an example of a "hybrid" distractor using repetition of a question word and a similar-sounding word.

A set of responses may use more than one type of distractor at a time. Not all distractors fit neatly into the categories outlined above; some may seem to belong to more than one category. Note also that each of these distractor types is similar because, in the end, they are inappropriate responses to the question or statement.

However, it is useful to look at *why* they are inappropriate and to understand what it is you must listen for.

Similar-Sounding Words

This type of distractor uses words and phrases that sound similar to the expected correct response. For example, you will hear:

> Man: *How many pairs of tickets do we need?*
>
> Narrator: *A.*
>
> Woman: *I eat chicken two or three times a week.*
>
> Narrator: *B.*
>
> Woman: *Four should be enough.*
>
> Narrator: *C.*
>
> Woman: *Get some pears, some apples, and some cherries, too.*

The correct response is (B): *Four should be enough.*

Choice (A) uses the word *eat*, which sounds a little like *need*, and *chicken*, which sounds a little like *ticket*. This is an example of a "similar-sound" distractor. (C) uses the word *pears*, which sounds like the word *pairs*. This is another example of a "similar-sound" distractor.

Repetition of Question Words

This type of distractor repeats words and phrases used in the question or statement.

You will hear:

Man:	*Are there any more copies of the annual report left?*
Narrator:	*A.*
Woman:	*Yes, there should be a few left on the shelf in the library.*
Narrator:	*B.*
Woman:	*No, I'm afraid he left early this afternoon.*
Narrator:	*C.*
Woman:	*Yes, turn left at the next traffic light.*

The correct response is (A): *Yes, there should be a few left on the shelf in the library.*

Choice (B) repeats the question word *left*, but here it has a different meaning. This is an example of a "repetition" distractor. (C) repeats the question word *left*, but, again, it has a different meaning. This is another example of a "repetition" distractor.

Irrelevant Responses

This type of distractor responds to a common misunderstanding of the question or statement.

You will hear:

Woman:	*Where will you stay when you go to London?*
Narrator:	*A.*
Man:	*I'm leaving on the tenth.*
Narrator:	*B.*
Man:	*At my cousin's house.*
Narrator:	*C.*
Man:	*Yes, I'm going there for a conference.*

The correct response is choice (B): *At my cousin's house.*

Choice (A) answers the question, *When will you go to London?* (C) answers the *Yes /No* question, *Will you go to London?* Both (A) and (C) are "irrelevant response" distractors.

Hybrid Distractors

This type of distractor uses combinations of the first 3 distractor types.

You will hear:

Man:	*When's the deadline for submitting contract bids?*
Narrator:	*A.*
Woman:	*They need to be in by five PM on Friday.*
Narrator:	*B.*
Woman:	*No, not until all the contract bids are in.*
Narrator:	*C.*
Woman:	*You can submit your contact information by e-mail.*

The correct response is (A): *They need to be in by five PM on Friday.*

Choice (B) repeats the question words *contract bids,* and it uses the word *until*, which might be expected in a response to a *When* question. The response is also a *Yes/No* answer to an information question. This distractor is a "hybrid" distractor combining repetition and an irrelevant response.

Choice (C) repeats the question word *submit*, and it uses the word *contact,* which sounds similar to *contract.* It also uses the phrase *by e-mail,* because an expected response to a *When* question often takes the form of *by + time word.* This is an example of a "hybrid" distractor using repetition and similar-sounding words.

STRATEGY 4: FOCUS ON THE PURPOSE OF THE QUESTION OR STATEMENT

Listen carefully to the question or statement that the first speaker makes. What is the intent of the first speaker? What kind of response does the speaker expect? Should the response be *Yes* or *No*? Should the response provide new information? Should the response indicate an opinion or offer advice?

Listen especially to the first word for clues as to whether the question is *Yes/No* or *Wh-information*. Knowing the intent of the first speaker is a key step in the process of choosing the correct response.

STRATEGY 5: EVALUATE THE STATEMENTS YOU HEAR AND MARK THE ANSWER IF YOU KNOW IT

Listen closely to the first word to determine what kind of question it is and to decide what the speaker's intent is. Once you know the intent of the question or statement, you must listen to and evaluate the responses you hear. Because each response will be spoken only once, you must listen carefully.

Listen for a response that closely matches the intent of the question. After you hear a statement that is a close match to the answer you have been expecting, find the number for the question on your answer sheet and mark the oval for the letter that matches your answer. Be sure to fill in your oval completely, as shown in the directions.

Be sure to listen to all 3 responses before you mark you answer sheet.

STRATEGY 6: ELIMINATE STATEMENTS THAT DO NOT FIT THE SITUATION AND SELECT THE BEST MATCH FROM WHAT IS LEFT

What if none of the responses match your expected answer very well? You must eliminate any choices that do not fit the situation.

Listen carefully to the first word to determine what kind of question it is. Eliminate any answers that are inappropriate. For example, eliminate a *Yes* or *No* answer to an information question.

Listen carefully to the tense used in the question and in the responses. Eliminate any answer choices that use the wrong tense; for example, a past tense response to a question about a future action.

If you must guess, eliminate the answer choices that repeat words from the question. Very often, these are distractors. Not always, but often.

STRATEGY 7: ANSWER THE CURRENT QUESTION BEFORE THE NEXT QUESTION BEGINS

Make sure you answer every question as quickly as you can. You have only about 8 seconds to choose your answer for each question or statement. You should be finished with the current question before the next one begins. If you are still answering a question when the next one begins, you might not hear the beginning of the question.

As soon as you have finished with a question, get ready to listen for the next one.

STRATEGY SUMMARY FOR PART 2

- Know the directions.

- Know the different kinds of question types.

- Understand the basic types of distractors.

- Focus on the purpose of the question or statement.

- Evaluate the statements you hear and mark the answer if you know it.

- Eliminate statements that do not fit the situation and select the best match from what is left.

- Be sure to answer the current question before the next question begins.

PRACTICE QUESTIONS

On the exam, *you will not be able to see the questions or the response*. They will be spoken, and you will hear them only once. Following are examples of the kinds of question–response items that will appear.

Directions

Read the question and the responses and mark the choice that best answers the question.

Practice 1

Man: *How many more Model X27s do we have left in stock?*

Narrator: A.

Woman: *That's right, it's the latest model.*

Narrator: B.

Woman: *That's a lot more than I thought we had.*

Narrator: C.

Woman: *No more than two dozen.*

Mark Your Answer:

Practice 2

Woman: *Shouldn't someone from the legal team sit in on the contract talks?*

Narrator: *A.*

Man: *I think the manager of the accounting team was there.*

Narrator: *B.*

Man: *There's been some talk of a merger, but I don't believe it.*

Narrator: *C.*

Man: *I've already asked Tom Brown to join us.*

Mark Your Answer: (A) (B) (C) (D)

Practice 3

Man: *Phillip Seymor wasn't at the meeting, was he?*

Narrator: *A.*

Woman: *No, he didn't.*

Narrator: *B.*

Woman: *No, he wasn't.*

Narrator: *C.*

Woman: *Yes, he has.*

Mark Your Answer: (A) (B) (C) (D)

Practice 4

Woman: *Will the equipment work in extreme cold?*

Narrator: *A.*

Man: *It's guaranteed to operate at temperatures as low as thirty below zero.*

Narrator: *B.*

Man: *I agree, it's very cold in here – I'll turn up the heat.*

Narrator: *C.*

Man: *I can, but I prefer to work with people, rather than with equipment.*

Mark Your Answer:　Ⓐ　Ⓑ　Ⓒ　Ⓓ

ANSWERS AND EXPLANATIONS

Practice 1

How many more Model X27s do we have left in stock?

- (A) That's right, it's the latest model.
- (B) That's a lot more than I thought we had.
- (C) No more than two dozen.

Explanation: The correct answer is Choice (C). (A) repeats the question word *model,* and uses the word *right* as the opposite of *left,* although the meaning of *left* in the question is different. It is also a *Yes/No* answer to a *Wh-information* question. This is an example of a "hybrid similar-sound and irrelevant response" distractor. (B) repeats the question word *more.* It also does not answer the question "How many?" This is an example of a "hybrid similar-sound and irrelevant response" distractor.

Practice 2

Shouldn't someone from the legal team sit in on the contract talks?

- (A) I think the manager of the accounting team was there.
- (B) There's been some talk of a merger, but I don't believe it.
- (C) I've already asked Tom Brown to join us.

Explanation: The correct answer is Choice (C). (A) does not answer the question. It is an example of an "irrelevant response" distractor. (B) repeats the question word *talk* but does not answer the question. This is an example of a "hybrid repetition and irrelevant response" distractor.

Practice 3

Phillip Seymor wasn't at the meeting, was he?

    (A) No, he didn't.

    (B) No, he wasn't.

    (C) Yes, he has.

Explanation: The correct answer is Choice (B). (A) and (C) use the wrong verbs. The tag question verb must match the auxiliary verb. This is an example of an "irrelevant response" distractor.

Practice 4

Will the equipment work in extreme cold?

    (A) It's guaranteed to operate at temperatures as low as thirty below zero.

    (B) I agree, it's very cold in here – I'll turn up the heat.

    (C) I can, but I prefer to work with people, rather than with equipment.

Explanation: The correct answer is Choice (A). (B) repeats the question word *cold* but does not answer the question. This is an example of a "hybrid repetition and irrelevant response" distractor. (C) repeats the question word *equipment* but does not answer the question. This is an example of a "hybrid repetition and irrelevant response" distractor.

Part 3: Short Conversations

On the third part of the TOEIC exam, you will hear a series of 10 short conversations between 2 people. Each conversation is followed by 3 questions, and each question has 4 answer choices. You must select the best answer choice for each question. The conversations are not printed in your test book, and because they are spoken only once, you must listen carefully. The questions will also be spoken only once, and they are also printed in your test book. The answer choices are also printed in your test book, but they are *not* spoken. Only the questions are spoken.

STRATEGY 1: KNOW THE DIRECTIONS

It is important to understand what you are being asked to do, and to be sure you know the directions before you take the test.

The directions for Part 3 will look like this:

> **Directions:** You will now hear a number of conversations between two people. You will be asked to answer three questions about what the speakers say. Select the best response to each question and mark the letter on your answer sheet. The conversations will be spoken only once and will not be printed in your test book.

Note that ETS does not provide a sample question for Part 3 in the test book.

Here is an example illustrating the format of a typical Part 3 Short Conversation and the 3 questions that follow.

You will hear:

> Narrator: *Questions 41 through 43 refer to the following conversation.*
>
> Woman: *Something smells delicious in here ... what is it?*
>
> Man: *It's vegetable lasagna. I made it for dinner last night. I made too much, and there's a lot left over, so I brought some for today's lunch.*
>
> Woman: *Well, it really does smell wonderful. How did you learn to make this?*
>
> Man: *It's my mother's family recipe—she got it from her grandmother. I'd be happy to bring it in to work tomorrow, if you'd like.*
>
> Narrator: *Number 41. What are the speakers mainly discussing?*

You will be able to read the first question and the 4 answer choices in your test book:

> 41. What are the speakers mainly discussing?
>
>   (A) The man's family
>   (B) A problem the woman has
>   (C) The food the man has made
>   (D) The restaurants in the area

There will be an 8-second pause after the first question. Then you will hear:

> Narrator: *Number 42. What does the man offer to do for the woman?*

You will be able to read the second question and the 4 answer choices in your test book:

---

42. What does the man offer to do for the woman?

    (A) Take her to lunch

    (B) Bring her his recipe

    (C) Introduce her to his family

    (D) Drive her to work the next day

There will be an 8-second pause after the second question. Then you will hear:

Narrator: *Number 43. What is probably true about the speakers?*

You will be able to read the third question and the 4 answer choices in your test book:

---

43. What is probably true about the speakers?

    (A) They are neighbors.

    (B) They are coworkers.

    (C) They are in a restaurant.

    (D) They are talking on the telephone.

Each question is spoken once, followed by an 8-second pause. This means for each question you have only 8 seconds to read the question and answer choices and mark your answer sheet.

The format of most of the short conversations is like the example above. Usually, there are 2 speakers, and you will hear each speaker twice; each speaker has 2 "turns" at speaking. This is the 4-line format. Occasionally, however, you will hear the second speaker only once; this is the 3-line format.

Part 3 Short Conversations—2 Formats	
4-line format	**3-line format**
Speaker A	Speaker A
Speaker B	Speaker B
Speaker A	Speaker A
Speaker B	

Almost all the short conversations are in the 4-line format. Both formats (4-line and 3-line) are followed by 3 questions.

STRATEGY 2: READ THE FIRST FEW QUESTIONS WHILE THE DIRECTIONS ARE PLAYING

Because you already know what the directions are, you should look at the first few questions in your test book while the directions are playing. This will let you know what to expect and what you will need to listen for.

Because the directions for Part 3 are short, there is not much time to read ahead. However, you should try to read as many questions as you can.

STRATEGY 3: UNDERSTAND QUESTION TYPES AND HOW QUESTIONS ARE ORDERED

In Part 3, the questions usually ask for information in the order in which it was presented in the conversation. This means that the first question will usually ask about something mentioned near the beginning, the second question will ask about something that was mentioned in the middle, and the third question will ask about something mentioned near the end.

There are 3 basic categories of questions for Part 3:

1. **Gist**

   Gist questions will ask what the main topic is, where the conversation takes place, or who the speakers are. They ask about the overall situation, rather than about specific details. Common Gist questions include:

   What are the speakers mainly discussing?

   Where does this conversation probably take place?

   Where do the speakers probably work?

   Who are the speakers?

2. **Detail**

   Detail questions ask about details mentioned in the conversation, such as what someone did or has been asked to do; how a problem is being handled; or the order in which things are to be done. They can ask about general information or very specific details. Common Detail questions include:

   What did the man do?

   What did the woman ask the man to do?

   How did the speakers solve their problem?

   Which will the man do first?

   When is the report due?

3. Implication/Inference

Implication/Inference questions ask about things that are not stated directly by either of the speakers. They can ask about the speakers' intentions, emotions, expectations, or probable future actions. Common Implication/Inference questions include:

What does the woman intend to do next week?

Why is the man disappointed?

What does the woman expect the man to do?

What will the man probably do next?

Some Implication/Inference questions and Gist questions may seem to be similar. For example, a Gist question that asks about where the conversation takes place requires an inference: The conversation will provide enough information to make the location or setting of the conversation obvious, but this information will not be stated directly. However, while some Gist questions require you to understand an implication or make an inference, Gist questions focus on the larger picture or the overall situation. Implication/Inference questions deal with details about the speakers or the situation.

COMMON PART 3 QUESTION PATTERNS

The most common patterns for Part 3 questions are:

A	B	C
Gist	Gist	Detail
Detail	Detail	Detail
Implication/Inference	Detail	Detail

Other patterns are possible, but these are the 3 most common.

Gist questions are often the first question, and Implication/Inference questions are often the last question.

Detail questions are asked in the order in which the information is presented in the conversation; for example, if there are 2 Detail questions, the first will ask about information presented near the beginning or middle of the conversation and the second will ask about information presented in the middle or at the end of the conversation.

STRATEGY 4: UNDERSTAND THE BASIC TYPES OF DISTRACTORS

To understand the kinds of Part 3 distractors and how they work, you first need to understand how ETS writes test items.

All Part 3 distractors must answer the question *plausibly*, that is, they must be possible answers to the question. When you look at a Part 3 question and the answer choices by themselves—without hearing the conversation—each choice must answer the question in a logical and realistic way. For example:

What did the man do on Monday?

(A) He left work early.

(B) He finished a report.

(C) He ate lunch at his desk.

(D) He replied to John's e-mail.

Without hearing the conversation, none of the answer choices can be eliminated. Each option is a plausible answer to the question, and there are no "impossible" answer choices. All Part 3 items are written in this way.

Another feature of Part 3 items is that none of the questions are "linked" in any way. That is, the information contained in a set of question and answer choices will not help you to answer any other questions.

There are four basic types of distractors for Part 3 items:

1. **Not Mentioned**

    This type of distractor uses words, phrases, and ideas that are not mentioned in the conversation. There is no connection to the language used in the conversation. The distractor answers the question plausibly but does not relate to the conversation.

2. **Repeated Words**

    This type of distractor uses words, phrases, and ideas that are mentioned in the conversation but changes them so that they are not true. The distractor answers the question plausibly but is incorrect.

3. **New Words**

    This type of distractor introduces new words, phrases, or ideas that may be associated with or implied by language and ideas expressed in the conversation but that are untrue. The distractor answers the question plausibly but is incorrect.

4. **Rephrase/Paraphrase**

    This type of distractor takes the original language used in the conversation and rephrases or paraphrases it in a way that makes it untrue. The distractor answers the question plausibly but is incorrect.

Note that a set of answer choices may use more than one type of distractor at a time. Not all distractors fit neatly into the categories outlined above; some may seem to belong to more than one category. Note also that each of these distractor types is similar because, in the end, they are incorrect answers to the question. However, it is useful to look at *why* they are incorrect and to understand what you must listen for.

Each distractor type will be discussed separately on the following pages.

Look at the Part 3 directions example again. (Material in *italics* indicates what you will hear; material in **bold** indicates what is printed in your test book.)

Narrator: *Questions 41 through 43 refer to the following conversation.*

Woman: *Something smells delicious in here ... what is it?*

Man: *It's vegetable lasagna. I made it for dinner last night. I made too much and there's a lot left over, so I brought some for today's lunch.*

Woman: *Well, it really does smell wonderful. How did you learn to make this?*

Man: *It's my mother's family recipe – she got it from her grandmother. I'd be happy to bring it in to work tomorrow, if you'd like.*

Narrator: *Number 41. What are the speakers mainly discussing?*

41. What are the speakers mainly discussing?

    (A) The man's family

    (B) A problem the woman has

    (C) The food the man has made

    (D) The restaurants in the area

This is a Gist question. The correct answer is Choice (C).

Choice (A) uses words, phrases, and ideas mentioned in the conversation (*mother, family, grandmother*), but the main topic of discussion is not the man's family. This is an example of a "repeated words" distractor.

Choice (B) is not mentioned or implied. This is an example of a "not mentioned" distractor.

Choice (D) is not mentioned, but uses the word *restaurant,* which is associated with the topics of food and cooking. This is an example of a "new words" distractor.

Narrator: *Number 42. What does the man offer to do for the woman?*

42. **What does the man offer to do for the woman?**

    (A) Take her to lunch
    (B) Bring her his recipe
    (C) Introduce her to his family
    (D) Drive her to work the next day

This is a "detail" question. The correct answer is Choice (B).

Choice (A) repeats the conversation word *lunch,* but the man has not offered to take the woman to lunch. This is an example of a "repeated words" distractor.

Choice (C) repeats the conversation word *family*, which is also associated with the conversation words *mother* and *grandmother.* This is an example of a "repeated words" distractor but could also be seen as a "rephrase/paraphrase" distractor.

Choice (D) plays on a rephrasing or paraphrasing of *"I'd be happy to bring it in to work tomorrow . . . ."* The man offers to bring his recipe to work the next day, not drive the woman. This is an example of a "rephrase/paraphrase" distractor.

Narrator: *Number 43. What is probably true about the speakers?*

43. What is probably true about the speakers?

    (A) They are neighbors.

    (B) They are coworkers.

    (C) They are in a restaurant.

    (D) They are talking on the telephone.

This is an Inference/Implication question. The correct answer is Choice is (B).

Choice (A) is not mentioned or implied and is an example of a "not mentioned" distractor.

Choice (C) is not mentioned, but it uses the word *restaurant,* which is associated with the topics of food and cooking. This is an example of a "new words" distractor.

Choice (D) is not mentioned or implied. Because the woman can smell the food, they must be in the same room at the same time. This is an example of a "not mentioned" distractor.

Notice that for each question, all the distractors are plausible answers, and that none of the questions or answer choices are of any help in answering other questions.

STRATEGY 5: LISTEN FOR THE INFORMATION IN THE QUESTIONS

By reading the questions in your test book, you will know what information to listen for in the conversation. For example, if the first question is a detail question asking about what one of the speakers has done, you should listen carefully for words and phrases that indicate what that speaker has done.

The conversations will often contain a lot of information that is *not* tested. However, because you have the questions in front of you in your test book, you will know what information to be listening for.

Note that the questions for Part 3 are all *Wh-* Information Questions. There are no *Yes/No* questions. Review the Part 2 Question—Response *Wh-* Information Question material to help you focus on the kinds of information the questions ask for and on the format of the expected answers. You should know, for example, that a *When* question deals with time and that you will need to listen for time words (e.g., *today, yesterday, this afternoon, at 10 o'clock*).

You will have to listen carefully to the conversation to get information you need. You will not be able to read the questions and apply logic to answer the questions. Remember, the question and answer choices used in one question will *not* help you to answer another question. The ETS test writers are very careful to avoid letting the information in one question and answer choice set help to answer another question and answer choice set.

Pay attention to who each speaker is. Often, the relationship between the speakers is made very clear, and there may be a question to test whether you understood this information. Sometimes the distractors will use information that is true for one of the speakers but not the other. For example, a man and woman might be discussing the man's vacation plans. For the question "*What are the speakers mainly discussing?*" one of the distractors may refer to the woman's vacation plans.

STRATEGY 6: ANSWER EACH QUESTION IN YOUR OWN WORDS BEFORE READING THE CHOICES

Read each question and predict the answer in your own words *before* reading the answer choices. If you understand the conversation, you should be able to answer all the questions in your own words. For each question, your predicted answer—or one very closely matching it—should be among the answer choices. Remember, there are no "trick" questions on the test. All the information needed to answer the questions is presented in the conversation.

If you read the answer choices first without answering the question in your own words, you will be tempted to make the answer one of the distractors. It is much better to have your own idea about the correct answer first, *before* looking at the ETS answer choices.

STRATEGY 7: EVALUATE THE ANSWER CHOICES AND MARK THE ANSWER IF YOU KNOW IT

If one of the answer choices is a close match to the answer you expect, mark the oval for that letter. Be sure to fill in the oval completely, as shown in the directions.

If none of the responses match your expected answer very well, you must eliminate as many choices as you can. Remember, one question and answer choice set will not help you answer another, so do not look at answer choices from one question for clues to answer another question.

Often, each answer choice uses words and phrases as they were spoken in the conversation. However, if only one of the answer choices uses words and phrases from the conversation, this is likely to be the correct one.

STRATEGY 8: ELIMINATE ANSWER CHOICES THAT ARE WRONG AND SELECT THE BEST MATCH FROM WHAT IS LEFT

What if none of the answer choices match your expected answer very well? In this case you must eliminate as many wrong choices as you can.

If you must guess, eliminate any choices that do not use words and phrases from the conversation—the "not mentioned" distractor type. (Unless there is only *one* choice that uses words and phrases from the conversation, in which case you should choose this as the correct answer.) The "not mentioned" distractors are often the easiest to eliminate.

STRATEGY 9: MANAGE YOUR TIME AND BE SURE TO ANSWER ALL THREE QUESTIONS BEFORE THE NEXT CONVERSATION BEGINS

Remember that there are only 8 seconds between questions. There is also an 8-second pause between the end of the last question and the introduction for the next conversation. If you spend too much time on one set of questions, you may miss the beginning of the next conversation. You will need to select your answer choice and mark it on your answer sheet as quickly as you can to keep up with the test. Because you will hear the conversations only once, you must not allow yourself to fall behind.

If you find yourself running out of time, mark your answer sheet with your "wild guess" letter. (See on page 15, **Strategy 7: Answer every question; choose one letter to use for all "wild guesses."**) Do not leave any questions unanswered.

STRATEGY 10: READ THE QUESTIONS FOR THE NEXT CONVERSATION BEFORE IT STARTS

For each conversation, there is a brief introduction. For example, you will hear: "*Questions 44 through 46 refer to the following conversation.*" Ideally, you should have answered all 3 questions for the current conversation before you hear the introduction for the next conversation. You should then immediately begin to read as many of the next set of questions as you can before the conversation begins. This will help you focus on the information you need to listen for.

PART 3 STRATEGY SUMMARY

- Know the directions.

- Read the first few questions while the directions are playing.

- Understand the question types and how questions are ordered.

- Understand the basic types of distractors.

- Listen for the information in the questions.

- Answer each question in your own words before reading the choices.

- Evaluate the answer choices and mark the answer if you know it.

- Eliminate answer choices that are wrong and select the best match from what is left.

- Manage your time and be sure to answer all 3 questions before the next conversation begins.

- Read the questions for the next conversation before it starts.

PRACTICE QUESTIONS

Note that during the exam *you will not be able to read the text for the conversations*. They will each be spoken, and you will hear them only once. The questions will also be spoken once, and you will be able to read them in your test book. The answer choices will be printed in your test book and are not spoken.

Following are examples of the kinds of Short Conversation items that will appear on Part 3 of the TOEIC exam. Answers and explanations start on page 108.

Directions

Read each conversation and the questions that follow. For each question, mark the choice that best answers the question.

Practice 1

Narrator: *Questions 1 through 3 refer to the following conversation.*

Man: *Hello Susan, this is John Davidson. I'm going to be in Los Angeles all next week, and I was wondering if you might have some time then to meet in person. I thought this might be a good opportunity for us to get acquainted face-to-face.*

Woman: *Hi John. Yes, I think it would be great if we could finally meet each other. Unfortunately, my schedule for next week is pretty full. The only time I have open is Wednesday between three and four. Does that work for you?*

Man: *Yes, that's perfect. I have a meeting with another client not too far from your office. I should be out of there by two or two-thirty. Shall we say three o'clock at your office?*

Woman: *That sounds good. I'm looking forward to meeting you!*

Narrator: *Number 1. What is true about the speakers?*

1. What is true about the speakers?

   (A) They have never met before.
   (B) They work for the same company.
   (C) They are traveling to Los Angeles together.
   (D) They are preparing to make a business presentation.

   Mark Your Answer:

Narrator: *Number 2. What is the man going to do before he meets the woman?*

2. What is the man going to do before he meets the woman?

   (A) Check his schedule
   (B) Go back to his office
   (C) Prepare some documents
   (D) Meet with another client

   Mark Your Answer:

Narrator: *Number 3. When will the speakers meet?*

3. When will the speakers meet?

   (A) 9:00 AM
   (B) 10:00 AM
   (C) 2:30 PM
   (D) 3:00 PM

Mark Your Answer:

Practice 2

Narrator: *Questions 4 through 6 refer to the following conversation.*

Woman: *As you know, nearly a third of our online customers are located in Korea. I think it might be a good idea to open some physical stores there.*

Man: *I'm not so sure. It's expensive to open up stores overseas; there's a lot of paperwork to fill out— you can't just go over there and open a store. We'd have to scout for locations . . . and then there's the problem of finding local staff . . . I'm not convinced that going through all that trouble would be worth it.*

Woman: *You make some good points. And I'm not saying it would be cheap or easy to do, but the number of Koreans buying from us online has been growing rapidly in each of the past six fiscal quarters. If we had a physical presence in Seoul, or one of the other big cities, we'd be able to process orders*

> *more quickly and offer better customer service.*
> *Our sales would definitely increase. I think we*
> *need to look into opening stores there.*

Man: *Maybe. But I'd like to see some hard data. Can*
you put together a report that makes the case?

Narrator: *Number 4. What does the woman think the company should do?*

4. What does the woman think the company should do?

   (A) Open stores in Korea

   (B) Find ways to cut costs

   (C) Move its main offices to Seoul

   (D) Change the way it sells products online

Mark Your Answer: (A)   (B)   (C)   (D)

Narrator: *Number 5. What claim does the woman make?*

5. What claim does the woman make?

   (A) Hiring local staff will be cheaper.

   (B) A third of online sales are to Koreans.

   (C) The Korean stores are the most profitable.

   (D) Online sales have increased by 60%.

Mark Your Answer: (A)   (B)   (C)   (D)

Narrator: *Number 6. What does the man ask the woman to do?*

6. What does the man ask the woman to do?

   (A) Scout locations in Korea

   (B) Prepare a detailed report

   (C) Look into hiring more local staff

   (D) Discuss her plan with the sales director

Mark Your Answer: Ⓐ   Ⓑ   Ⓒ   Ⓓ

Practice 3

Narrator: *Questions 7 through 9 refer to the following conversation.*

Man A: *What did you think about the Allied Micronics presentation?*

Man B: *Honestly? I thought it was terrible. They seemed totally unprepared. They clearly don't understand what our business is. What they were talking about was pretty irrelevant to what we do. I was surprised at how little research they did.*

Man A: *I'm glad to hear you say that because I agree completely. It's as if they hadn't read our proposal specifications.*

Man B: *I guess they don't really need our contract. Let's hope the other companies that responded are better prepared!*

Narrator: *Number 7. What are the speakers mainly discussing?*

7. What are the speakers mainly discussing?

   (A) A contract change
   (B) A business presentation
   (C) Who should get a contract
   (D) How to respond to a customer

Mark Your Answer:

Narrator: *Number 8. Why are the speakers surprised?*

8. Why are the speakers surprised?

   (A) Allied Micronics did not win the contract.
   (B) Allied Micronics did not submit a bid proposal.
   (C) Allied Micronics did not prepare for the presentation.
   (D) Allied Micronics did not tell them about the new specifications.

Mark Your Answer:

Narrator: *Number 9. What can be inferred about the speakers?*

9. What can be inferred about the speakers?

   (A) They work for Allied Micronics.
   (B) They are talking on the telephone.
   (C) They plan to rewrite their contract proposal.
   (D) They will meet with representatives from other companies.

Mark Your Answer:

KAPLAN

ANSWERS AND EXPLANATIONS

Practice 1

Narrator: *Questions 1 through 3 refer to the following conversation.*

Man: *Hello Susan, this is John Davidson. I'm going to be in Los Angeles all next week, and I was wondering if you might have some time then to meet in person. I thought this might be a good opportunity for us to get acquainted face-to-face.*

Woman: *Hi John. Yes, I think it would be great if we could finally meet each other. Unfortunately, my schedule for next week is pretty full. The only time I have open is Wednesday between three and four. Does that work for you?*

Man: *Yes, that's perfect. I have a meeting with another client not too far from your office. I should be out of there by two or two-thirty. Shall we say three o'clock at your office?*

Woman: *That sounds good. I'm looking forward to meeting you!*

1. What is true about the speakers?

   (A) They have never met before.
   (B) They work for the same company.
   (C) They are traveling to Los Angeles together.
   (D) They are preparing to make a business presentation.

> *the other big cities, we'd be able to process orders more quickly and offer better customer service. Our sales would definitely increase. I think we need to look into opening stores there.*

Man: *Maybe. But I'd like to see some hard data. Can you put together a report that makes the case?*

4. What does the woman think the company should do?

(A) Open stores in Korea
(B) Find ways to cut costs
(C) Move its main offices to Seoul
(D) Change the way it sells products online

Explanation: The correct answer is Choice (A). This is a Gist question. The woman says, *I think it might be a good idea to open some physical stores there,* and *I think we need to look into opening stores there.*

Choice (B) is not mentioned. It uses the word *costs,* which is associated with the words *expensive* and *cheap* used in the conversation, but the woman does not say anything about cutting costs.

Choice (C) repeats the word *Seoul*, but the woman does not say the company should move its main offices there.

Choice (D) repeats the word *online* and uses the word *sell*, which is associated with *sales* and other ideas expressed in the conversation; however, the woman does not say anything about changing the way the company sells online.

5. What claim does the woman make?

(A) Hiring local staff will be cheaper.

(B) A third of online sales are to Koreans.

(C) The Korean stores are the most profitable.

(D) Online sales have increased by 60%.

Explanation: The correct answer is Choice (B). This is a Detail question. The woman says, *Nearly a third of our online customers are located in Korea.*

Choice (A) repeats the words *local staff*. The man mentions the need to hire local staff; the woman does not say hiring local staff will be cheaper.

Choice (C) is not mentioned.

Choice (D) is not mentioned. It is an incorrect paraphrase of the woman's statement: *The number of Koreans buying from us online has been growing rapidly in each of the past six fiscal quarters.*

6. What does the man ask the woman to do?

(A) Scout locations in Korea

(B) Prepare a detailed report

(C) Look into hiring more local staff

(D) Discuss her plan with the sales director

Explanation: The correct answer is Choice (B). This is a Detail question. The man asks the woman if she can *put together a report that makes the case,* meaning a report with details explaining why opening stores in Korea would be a good idea.

Choice (A) repeats the phrase *scout locations*, but the man does not ask the woman to do this.

Choice (C) repeats the phrase *local staff*, but the man does not ask the woman to do this.

Choice (D) is not mentioned.

Practice 3

Narrator: *Questions 7 through 9 refer to the following conversation*

Man A: *What did you think about the Allied Micronics presentation?*

Man B: *Honestly? I thought it was terrible. They seemed totally unprepared. They clearly don't understand what our business is. What they were talking about was pretty irrelevant to what we do. I was surprised at how little research they did.*

Man A: *I'm glad to hear you say that because I agree completely. It's as if they hadn't read our proposal specifications.*

Man B: *I guess they don't really need our contract. Let's hope the other companies that responded are better prepared!*

7. What are the speakers mainly discussing?

   (A) A contract change
   (B) A business presentation
   (C) Who should get a contract
   (D) How to respond to a customer

Explanation: The correct answer is Choice (B). This is a Gist question. The speakers are discussing a presentation made by Allied Micronics.

Choices (A) and (C) both repeat the word *contract*, but this is not the main topic of the conversation.

Choice (D) uses the word *responded*, but the speakers are not discussing responding to a customer.

8. Why are the speakers surprised?

   (A) Allied Micronics did not win the contract.
   (B) Allied Micronics did not submit a bid proposal.
   (C) Allied Micronics did not prepare for the presentation.
   (D) Allied Micronics did not tell them about the new specifications.

Explanation: The correct answer is Choice (C). This is a Detail question, but it is also a Gist question. One of the men says that he is *surprised at how little research they did*. This makes this a Detail question. At the same time, the overall theme of the conversation is the speakers' surprise at the quality of the presentation. This makes this a Gist question.

Choice (A) repeats the word *contract* but is incorrect.

Choice (B) repeats the word *proposal* but is incorrect.

Choice (D) repeats the word *specifications* but is incorrect.

9. What can be inferred about the speakers?

   (A) They work for Allied Micronics.
   (B) They are talking on the telephone.
   (C) They plan to rewrite their contract proposal.
   (D) They will meet with representatives from other companies.

Explanation: The correct answer is Choice (D). This is an Inference/Implication question. The conversations ends with one of the men saying, *Let's hope the other companies that responded are better prepared!* From this, we can reasonably infer that there will be other presentations made by other companies and that the men will meet with the representatives during the presentations.

Choice (A) is incorrect because the men have made clear that Allied Micronics is *not* the company they work for.

Choice (B) is not implied. We cannot be sure whether or not the men are talking to each other directly or whether or not they are talking on the telephone. It is not reasonable to infer that they are talking on the telephone.

Choice (C) is not implied. The words *contract* and *proposal* are repeated, but the men do not imply that they will rewrite anything.

Part 4. Short Talks

On the fourth part of the TOEIC exam, you will hear a series of 10 short talks, each spoken by just one speaker. Each talk is followed by 3 questions, and each question has 4 answer choices. You must select the best answer choice for each question. The talks are not printed in your test book—because they are spoken only once, you must listen carefully. The answer choices are printed in your test book, but they are *not* spoken. Only the questions are spoken.

The contexts for the talks are common situations where a speaker would directly address an audience of one or more people, such as a presentation, lecture, speech, or guided tour. The talks also include voice-mail messages, telephone menus, news reports, radio programs, and other kinds of recorded announcements.

Many of the strategies for handling Part 4 are very similar to those for handling Part 3.

STRATEGY 1: KNOW THE DIRECTIONS

It is important to understand what you are being asked to do and to be sure you know the directions before you take the test.

The directions for Part 4 will look like this:

Directions: You will now hear short talks given by a single speaker. You will be asked to answer three questions about what the speaker says. Select the best response to each question and mark the letter on your answer sheet. The talks will be spoken only once and will not be printed in your test book.

Note that ETS does not provide a sample question for Part 4 in the test book.

The following page is an example illustrating the format of a typical Part 4 Short Talk and the 3 questions that follow. You will hear:

Narrator: *Questions 71 through 73 refer to the following talk.*

Man: *Good morning everyone. Today I'd like to discuss our strategy for the New York City area. As I'm sure you're all aware, real estate prices there are among the highest in the nation and are continuing to rise. On the one hand, this is good news in the short term because it means that the company's rental properties there will continue to be profitable. On the other hand, if the trend continues, it means that acquiring and developing new residential and business properties will become more costly; and because rents are so high already, we won't be able to charge what we need to maintain our current return on investment—over time, returns will fall. There are also some signs that the New York market may be turning around—houses and apartments are staying on the market an average of two days longer now than they did six months ago. While sellers are still getting contracts at the prices they want, it's taking longer to get them. This could mean that housing prices and rents are poised to come down soon. The situation is rather mixed and difficult to read. What I'd like us to do is formulate a revised strategy that balances the*

You will be able to read the first question and the 4 answer choices in your test book:

---

71. What does the speaker say could happen if the current trend in real estate prices continues?

    (A) Return on investment could fall.
    (B) Development opportunities could increase.
    (C) Fewer residential properties could be available.
    (D) Selling commercial properties could become more difficult.

There will be an 8-second pause after the first question. Then you will hear:

Narrator: *Number 72. What does the speaker claim regarding New York City real estate?*

You will be able to read the second question and the 4 answer choices in your test book:

---

72. What does the speaker claim regarding New York City real estate?

    (A) Prices have fallen in the past six months.
    (B) Houses and apartments are taking longer to sell.
    (C) Apartment sales have doubled in the past six months.
    (D) Commercial properties are a good long-term investment.

There will be an 8-second pause after the second question. Then you will hear:

> Narrator: *Number 73. What does the speaker want to change?*

You will be able to read the third question and the 4 answer choices in your test book:

> 73. What does the speaker want to change?
>
> (A) A project schedule
> (B) A meeting agenda
> (C) A company strategy
> (D) A real estate contract

Each question is spoken once, followed by an 8-second pause. This means for each question you have only 8 seconds to read the question and answer choices and mark your answer sheet.

STRATEGY 2: READ THE FIRST FEW QUESTIONS WHILE THE DIRECTIONS ARE PLAYING

Because you already know what the directions are, you should look at the first few questions in your test book while the directions are playing—just as you did for Part 3. This will let you know what to expect and what you will need to listen for.

Because the directions for Part 4 are short, there is not much time to read ahead. However, you should try to read as many questions as you can.

STRATEGY 3: UNDERSTAND QUESTION TYPES AND HOW QUESTIONS ARE ORDERED

The organization of Part 4 questions is similar to that for Part 3. The questions generally ask for information in the order in which it is presented in the talk: The first question will usually ask about something mentioned near the beginning, the second question will ask about something mentioned in the middle, and the third question will ask about something mentioned near the end.

There are 3 basic categories of questions for Part 4. (These are essentially the same categories found in Part 3).

1. **Gist**

   Gist questions will ask what the main topic is, where the talk takes place, or who the intended audience is. Gist questions ask about the overall situation rather than about specific details. Here are some examples:

   Who is the speaker?

   Who is the intended audience?

   What is the speaker mainly discussing?

   What is the purpose of the announcement?

   Where does this talk probably take place?

2. **Detail**

   Detail questions ask about information mentioned in the talk. They can ask about general information or very specific details. Examples of what Detail questions might cover include what a speaker has said about something or someone; when an action or event will take place; what role, function, or responsibility people will have; how a problem or situation is being handled; the order in which things are to be done; or what products or services a company provides. Here are some examples:

   What does the speaker say about Starboard Enterprises?

   What will happen the next day?

   What will David Johnson's role be?

Where will the old files be kept?

When should the first locking nut be removed?

What service does Travis Consulting provide?

3. **Implication/Inference**

   Implication/Inference questions ask about things that are not stated directly by the speaker. They can ask about the speaker's intentions, emotions, expectations, or probable future actions. Common Implication/Inference questions include:

   What does the speaker intend to do next week?

   Why is the speaker surprised?

   What does the speaker expect managers to do?

   What will the speaker probably do next?

   What does the speaker imply about the new rules?

Some Implication/Inference questions and Gist questions might seem to be similar. For example, a Gist question that asks about who the talk is intended for requires an inference: The talk will provide enough information about the location, setting, or situation to make the intended audience obvious, but the identity of the audience will not likely be stated directly. However, while some Gist questions require you to understand an implication or make an inference, they generally focus on the larger picture or the overall situation. Implication/Inference questions tend to deal with implied details about something the speaker is discussing, expecting, planning, or intending to do, or about details that concern the situation or context itself.

COMMON PART 4 QUESTION PATTERNS

Part 4 questions patterns are essentially the same as those for Part 3. The most common patterns for Part 4 questions are:

A	B	C
Gist	Gist	Detail
Detail	Detail	Detail
Implication/Inference	Detail	Detail

Other patterns are possible, but these are the three most common.

Gist questions are often first, and Implication/Inference questions are often last.

As is the case for Part 3, Part 4 Detail questions are asked in the order in which the information is presented in the talk. For example, if there are 2 Detail questions, the first will ask about information presented near the beginning or middle of the talk, and the second will ask about information presented in the middle or at the end of the talk.

STRATEGY 4: UNDERSTAND THE BASIC TYPES OF DISTRACTORS

The distractors for Part 4 are essentially the same as those used in Part 3.

As was the case for Part 3, all Part 4 distractors will answer the question "plausibly," that is, they will be possible answers to the question. When you look at a set of Part 4 question and the answer choices by themselves—without hearing the talk—each choice will answer the question in a logical and realistic way, and no choice can be eliminated using logic or common sense. Each option will be a plausible answer to the question, and there are no "impossible" answer choices. All Part 4 items are written in this way.

As was described for Part 3, none of the Part 4 questions are "linked" in any way, that is, the information contained in a set of question and answer choices will not help you to answer any other questions.

There are four basic types of distractors for Part 4 items:

1. **Not Mentioned**

   This type of distractor uses words, phrases, and ideas that are not mentioned in the talk, but there is no connection to the language used in the talk. The distractor answers the question plausibly but does not relate to the talk.

2. **Repeated Words**

   This type of distractor uses words, phrases, and ideas that are mentioned in the talk, but it changes them so that they are not true. The distractor answers the question plausibly but is incorrect.

3. **New Words**

   This type of distractor introduces new words, phrases, or ideas that may be associated with or implied by language and ideas expressed in the talk, but that are untrue. The distractor answers the question plausibly but is incorrect.

4. **Rephrase/Paraphrase**

   This type of distractor takes the original language used in the talk and rephrases or paraphrases it in a way that makes it untrue. The distractor answers the question plausibly but is incorrect.

Note that a set of answer choices may use more than one type of distractor at a time. Not all distractors fit neatly into the categories outlined above; some may seem to belong to more than one category. Note also that each of these distractor types is similar because, in the end, they are incorrect answers to the question. However, it is useful to look at *why* they are incorrect and to understand what you must listen for.

Each distractor type will be discussed separately below.

Look at the Part 4 directions example again. (Material in *italics* indicates what you will hear; material in **bold** indicates what is printed in your test book.)

Narrator: *Questions 71 through 73 refer to the following talk.*

Man: *Good morning everyone. Today I'd like to discuss our strategy for the New York City area. As I'm sure you're all aware, real estate prices there are among the highest in the nation and are continuing to rise. On the one hand, this is good news in the short term because it means that the company's rental properties there will continue to be profitable. On the other hand, if the trend continues, it means that acquiring and developing new residential and business properties will become more costly; and because rents are so high already, we won't be able to charge what we need to maintain our current return on investment— over time, returns will fall. There are also some signs that the New York market may be turning around—houses and apartments are staying on the market an average of two days longer now than they did six months ago. While sellers are still getting contracts at the prices they want, it's taking longer to get them. This could mean that housing prices and rents are poised to come down soon. The situation is rather mixed and difficult to read. What I'd like us to do is formulate a revised strategy that balances the rewards we now enjoy in the current boom market against the future risks of a soft housing market.*

Narrator: *Number 71. What does the speaker say could happen if the current trend in real estate prices continues?*

---

71. What does the speaker say could happen if the current trend in real estate prices continues?

(A) Return on investment could fall.

(B) Development opportunities could increase.

(C) Fewer residential properties could be available.

(D) Selling commercial properties could become more difficult.

The correct answer is Choice (A). This is a Detail question.

Choice (B) uses the word *development* from the talk, but it also introduces the idea of an increase in development opportunities, which is not mentioned, and is therefore a false statement.

Choice (C) uses the words *residential properties* from the talk, but the idea that fewer of them will be available is not mentioned and is therefore incorrect.

Choice (D) uses words, phrases, and ideas mentioned or implied in the talk (*commercial properties, difficult*), but it rephrases them in a way that is not true.

Narrator: *Number 72. What does the speaker claim regarding New York City real estate?*

72. **What does the speaker claim regarding New York City real estate?**

    (A) Prices have fallen in the past six months.
    (B) Houses and apartments are taking longer to sell.
    (C) Apartment sales have doubled in the past six months.
    (D) Commercial properties are a good long-term investment.

The correct answer is Choice (B). This is a Detail question.

Choice (A) takes words, phrases, and ideas mentioned in the talk (*prices, fall, six months ago*) and rephrases them to make a false statement.

Choice (C) uses words from the talk (*apartment, six months ago*) but combines them in a way that is incorrect.

Choice (D) takes words, phrases, and ideas mentioned or implied in the conversation (*commercial properties, long-term investments, difficult*) and rephrases them to make a false statement.

Narrator: *Number 73. What does the speaker want to change?*

73. **What does the speaker want to change?**

    (A) A project schedule

    (B) A meeting agenda

    (C) A company strategy

    (D) A real estate contract

The correct answer is Choice (C). This is a Detail question.

Choice (A) is not mentioned or implied and is an example of a "not mentioned" distractor.

Choice (B) is not mentioned or implied and is an example of a "not mentioned" distractor.

Choice (D) repeats words and phrases from the talk (*real estate, contract*), but this is not what the speaker wants to change.

Notice that for each question all the distractors are plausible answers, and none of the questions or answer choices are of any help in answering other questions.

STRATEGY 5: LISTEN FOR THE INFORMATION IN THE QUESTIONS

As was described in Part 3, by reading the questions in your test book, you will know what information you need to be listening for. For example, if the first question is a Gist question asking about who the audience is, you should listen carefully for words and phrases that indicate where the talk takes place and who the audience is most likely to be.

The talks will often contain a lot of information that is *not* tested. However, because you are able to read the questions in your test book, you will know what information to be listening for, and you should focus on finding what you need to answer each question.

Note that the questions for Part 4 are all *Wh-* Information Questions—as was the case for Part 3. There are no *Yes/No* questions. Go back and review the Part 2 Question–Response *Wh-* Information Question material starting on page 50. Be sure you understand the kinds of information the question types ask for and the format of the expected answers. You should know, for example, that a *When* question deals with time and that you will need to listen for time words (e.g., *today, yesterday, this afternoon, at 10 o'clock*).

You will have to listen carefully to the talk to get information you need. Remember, the question and answer choices used in one question set will *not* help you to answer another question.

Pay attention to the context of the talk. Know who the speaker is and what his or her relationship to the audience is. Listen for clues that tell you where the talk is likely to take place. If a speaker is addressing an audience, the setting and relationship between the speaker and the audience is usually made very clear, and there is often a question that tests whether you have understood this.

Be sure you also understand the purpose of the talk. If a speaker is addressing an audience (making a business presentation, for example), understand why the speaker is addressing this particular audience. If an announcement is being made, listen for clues to its purpose to understand *why* the announcement is being made.

STRATEGY 6: ANSWER EACH QUESTION IN YOUR OWN WORDS BEFORE READING THE CHOICES

Read each question and predict the answer in your own words *before* reading the answer choices. If you understand the talk, you should be able to answer each question in your own words. Your predicted answer—or one very closely matching —should be among the answer choices. Remember, there are no "trick" questions on the test. All the information needed to answer the questions is presented in the talk.

It is much better to have your own idea about the correct answer first, *before* looking at the answer choices. If you look at the answer choices first, you might be attracted to an incorrect choice and wind up listening to the talk for that information, which might not even be mentioned.

STRATEGY 7: EVALUATE THE ANSWER CHOICES AND MARK THE ANSWER IF YOU KNOW IT

As you did with Part 3, find the answer choice that is a close match to the one you expect and mark your answer sheet. Be sure to fill in the oval completely, as shown in the test directions.

If no answer choice matches your expected answer very well, eliminate as many choices as you can. Remember, one question and answer choice set will not help you answer another; do not look at answer choices from one question for clues to answer another question.

Often, each answer choice uses words and phrases used in the talk. However, if there is only *one* answer choice that uses words and phrases from the talk, this is very likely the correct one.

STRATEGY 8: ELIMINATE ANSWER CHOICES THAT ARE WRONG AND SELECT THE BEST MATCH FROM WHAT IS LEFT

If none of the answer choices matches your expected answer very well, then you must eliminate as many wrong choices as you can.

If you find you have to guess, the same guessing strategy used for Part 3 works for Part 4, too. Eliminate any choices that do not use words and phrases from the talk—the "not mentioned" distractor type. (Unless there is only *one* choice that uses words and phrases from the talk—in which case you should choose this as the correct answer.) The "not mentioned" distractors are often the easiest to eliminate.

STRATEGY 9: MANAGE YOUR TIME AND BE SURE TO ANSWER ALL 3 QUESTIONS BEFORE THE NEXT TALK BEGINS

Remember that there are only 8 seconds between questions. There is also an 8-second pause between the end of the last question and the introduction for the next talk. You will need to work quickly to keep up with the test. You will hear the conversations only once. Do not waste time answering any individual question—you risk missing the beginning of the next talk, which could contain information you need to answer the questions that follow. Select your answer choice and mark it on your answer sheet as quickly as you can.

If you find yourself running out of time, mark your answer sheet with your "wild guess" letter. (See on page 15: **Strategy 7: Answer every question; choose one letter to use for all "wild guesses."**) Do not leave any questions unanswered.

STRATEGY 10: READ THE QUESTIONS FOR THE NEXT TALK BEFORE IT STARTS

Just as each Part 3 Conversation had a brief introduction; each Part 4 Talk does too. For example, you will hear:

> Questions 71 through 73 refer to the following voicemail message.

You should try to answer all 3 questions for the current talk before you hear the introduction for the next talk. Then, while the introduction is playing, begin immediately to read as many of the next set of questions as you can before the actual talk begins. This will help you focus on what information you need to listen for.

PART 4 STRATEGY SUMMARY

- Know the directions.

- Read the first few questions while the directions are playing.

- Understand question types and how questions are ordered.

- Understand the basic types of distractors.

- Listen for the information in the questions.

- Answer each question in your own words before reading the choices.

- Evaluate the answer choices and mark the answer if you know it.

- Eliminate answer choices that are wrong and select the best match from what is left.

- Manage your time and be sure to answer all 3 questions before the next talk begins.

- Read the questions for the next talk before it starts.

PRACTICE QUESTIONS

Note that during the exam, *you will not be able to read the text for the talks.* They will each be spoken, and you will hear them only once. The questions will be spoken once, and you will be able to read them in your test book. The answer choices will be printed in your test book.

Following are examples of the kinds of Short Talk items that will appear on Part 4. Answers and explanations begin on page 141.

Directions

Read each talk and the questions that follow. For each question, mark the choice that best answers the question.

Practice 1

Narrator: *Questions 1 through 3 refer to the following talk.*

Man: *There have been a lot of rumors going around in recent weeks concerning the company's future. It's time you got the fact...effective August first, Kramer Enterprises will become the majority shareholder in our company. They will own fifty-eight percent of our stock and will thus have a controlling interest. We've had several meetings with Kramer's senior management team, and they've assured us that they do not plan to make any big changes to the way we do things and, most importantly, that there will be no layoffs. They plan to let us run the company pretty much as we have been, with the exception that our*

*accounting functions will now be handled by
Kramer's accounting department. This will mean
the elimination of our own accounting team, but
Kramer plans to absorb the current staff—you
won't be losing your jobs, but you'll be reassigned
and, possibly, be given new duties.*

Narrator: *Number 1. What is probably true about the
speaker's audience?*

1. What is probably true about the speaker's audience?

   (A) They are employees at his company.
   (B) They own the majority of his company's stock
       shares.
   (C) They have a controlling interest in Kramer
       Enterprises.
   (D) They are part of Kramer Enterprises' senior manage-
       ment team.

Mark Your Answer:

Narrator: *Number 2. What is learned about Kramer Enterprises?*

2. What is learned about Kramer Enterprises?

   (A) It does not plan to lay off workers.
   (B) It will close several branch offices.
   (C) It will make key changes to the way the company is run.
   (D) It does not plan to keep the current management team in place.

   Mark Your Answer: Ⓐ Ⓑ Ⓒ Ⓓ

Narrator: *Number 3. Which functions will be taken over by Kramer Enterprises?*

3. Which function(s) will be taken over by Kramer Enterprises?

   (A) Shipping
   (B) Accounting
   (C) Sales and Marketing
   (D) Research and Development

   Mark Your Answer: Ⓐ Ⓑ Ⓒ Ⓓ

Practice 2

Narrator: *Questions 4 through 6 refer to the following talk.*

Woman: *Good evening ladies and gentlemen, thank you all for coming. Welcome to The Laughing Goat Cafe's Poetry for the People open poetry reading. For those of you who have never been here before, here's how it works: Each Wednesday evening, we provide a venue for local poets to read their works before a live audience—that's you folks. We don't pay the poets to read, and we don't charge you to listen. This is free for everyone. All we ask is that you don't talk too loudly while the poets are reading, and that you turn your cell phones off. Okay, let's get started . . . We have 10 poets scheduled to read this evening, some of whom are regulars, plus a few first-timers as well. First up is one of our regulars, John Taylor. John is the owner of the Beatnik Bookstore, and he teaches writing and poetry workshops at the Downtown Community College. He has published a collection of short stories, and his poems appear regularly in Contemporary Poetry magazine and in Rhyme Time Monthly. Ladies and gentlemen, please welcome John Taylor.*

Narrator: *Number 4. On which day are the poetry readings held?*

4. On which day are the poetry readings held?

(A) Mondays

(B) Wednesdays

(C) Saturdays

(D) Sundays

Mark Your Answer:

Narrator: *Number 5. What is learned about the poetry readings?*

5. What is learned about the poetry readings?

(A) They often sell out.

(B) They cost nothing to attend.

(C) They are popular with college students.

(D) They have been held each week for the past 10 years.

Narrator: *Number 6. Who is John Taylor?*

Mark Your Answer:

6. Who is John Taylor?

(A) The owner of the Laughing Goat Cafe

(B) A frequent participant at the poetry readings

(C) The publisher of *Contemporary Poetry* magazine

(D) A first-time participant at the poetry readings

Mark Your Answer:

Practice 3

Narrator: *Questions 7 through 9 refer to the following talk.*

Man: *To help us keep better track of copier use, we're going to install a new Xcel 2000 photocopier, which is scheduled to arrive this weekend and will be ready for use on Monday. The new copier will have all the functions of the Xcel 1800 that we have now, but it will require you to enter a project authorization code, which you'll get from your project managers. So beginning next Monday, every time you need to make copies for a project you'll have to enter a code. You'll also be assigned a personal code, which you can use for general copying—but for work-related material only, of course. The reason we're doing this is to try and reign in overhead costs. Some projects require enormous numbers of photocopies. For example, we photocopied almost 50,000 pages for the MetaWorks project. We're going to allow each project up to 5,000 pages free, and then we'll bill the client for each page over that. By using project authorization codes, we'll be able to track each project's page count accurately.*

Narrator: *Number 7. When is a project code needed?*

7. When is a project code needed?

   (A) When ordering supplies

   (B) When filling out time sheets

   (C) When using the copy machine

   (D) When shipping packages overnight

Mark Your Answer:

Narrator: *Number 8. Who will give employees authorization codes?*

8. Who will give employees authorization codes?

   (A) MetaWorks

   (B) The speaker

   (C) Project managers

   (D) The human resources department

Mark Your Answer:

Narrator: *Number 9. When will employees begin using project codes?*

9. When will employees begin using project codes?

   (A) Later that day

   (B) The next day

   (C) The following Monday

   (D) In two weeks

Mark Your Answer:

ANSWERS AND EXPLANATIONS

Practice 1

Narrator: *Questions 1 through 3 refer to the following talk.*

Man: *There have been a lot of rumors going around in recent weeks concerning the company's future. It's time you got the fact…effective August first, Kramer Enterprises will become the majority shareholder in our company. They will own fifty-eight percent of our stock and will thus have a controlling interest. We've had several meetings with Kramer's senior management team, and they've assured us that they do not plan to make any big changes to the way we do things and, most importantly, that there will be no layoffs. They plan to let us run the company pretty much as we have been, with the exception that our accounting functions will now be handled by Kramer's accounting department. This will mean the elimination of our own accounting team, but Kramer plans to absorb the current staff—you won't be losing your jobs, but you'll be reassigned and, possibly, be given new duties.*

1. What is probably true about the speaker's audience?

   (A) They are employees at his company.
   (B) They own the majority of his company's stock shares.
   (C) They have a controlling interest in Kramer Enterprises.
   (D) They are part of Kramer Enterprises' senior management team.

Explanation: The correct answer is Choice (A). This is an Inference/Implication question. The speaker is clearly talking to employees. He refers to "our company" and to the audience as "you." It is strongly implied that the audience is a group of his employees.

Choice (B) rephrases language and ideas from the talk (*become the majority shareholder, own 58 percent of our stock*), but it does so incorrectly. It is Kramer Enterprises who will own the majority of the company's stock, not the audience.

Choice (C) repeats language and ideas from the talk (*have a controlling interest*), but the statement is incorrect. It is Kramer Enterprises who will have a controlling interest in the company, not the audience.

Choice (D) repeats language and ideas from the talk (*senior management team*), but the statement is incorrect. The speaker mentions Kramer Enterprises' senior management team.

2. What is learned about Kramer Enterprises?

   (A) It does not plan to lay off workers.
   (B) It will close several branch offices.
   (C) It will make key changes to the way the company is run.
   (D) It does not plan to keep the current management team in place.

Explanation: The correct answer is Choice (A). This is a Detail question. This is stated directly (*there will be no layoffs*).

Choice (B) is not mentioned.

Choice (C) rephrases words from the talk (*run the company, big changes to the way we do things*) but it alters them so that they are not true.

Choice (D) combines words and phrases from the talk (*They plan to, management team*) but the statement is not true.

3. Which functions will be taken over by Kramer Enterprises?

   (A) Shipping
   (B) Accounting
   (C) Sales and Marketing
   (D) Research and Development

Explanation: The correct answer is Choice (B). This is a Detail question. This is stated directly (*our accounting functions will now be handled by Kramer's accounting department*).

Choices (A), (C), and (D) are not mentioned.

Practice 2

Narrator: *Questions 4 through 6 refer to the following talk*

Woman: *Good evening ladies and gentlemen, thank you all for coming. Welcome to The Laughing Goat Cafe's Poetry for the People open poetry reading. For those of you who have never been here before, here's how it works: Each Wednesday evening, we provide a venue for local poets to read their works before a live audience—that's you folks. We don't pay the poets to read, and we don't charge you to listen. This is free for everyone. All we ask is that you don't talk too loudly while the poets are reading, and that you turn your cell phones off. Okay, let's get started . . . We have 10 poets scheduled to read this evening, some of whom are regulars, plus a few first-timers as well. First up is one of our regulars, John Taylor. John is the owner of the Beatnik Bookstore, and he teaches writing and poetry workshops at the Downtown Community College. He has published a collection of short stories, and his poems appear regularly in Contemporary Poetry magazine and in Rhyme Time Monthly. Ladies and gentlemen, please welcome John Taylor.*

4. On which day are the poetry readings held?

   (A) Mondays

   (B) Wednesdays

   (C) Saturdays

   (D) Sundays

Explanation: The correct answer is Choice (B). This is a Detail question. The speaker states this directly (*Each Wednesday evening, we provide a venue for local poets to read their works before a live audience—that's you folks.*).

Choices (A), (C), and (D) are not mentioned.

5. What is learned about the poetry readings?

   (A) They often sell out.

   (B) They cost nothing to attend.

   (C) They are popular with college students.

   (D) They have been held each week for the past 10 years.

Explanation: The correct answer is Choice (B). This is a Detail question. The speaker states this directly (*We don't pay the poets to read, and we don't charge you to listen. This is free for everyone.*).

Choice (A) is not mentioned.

Choice (C) repeats the word *college* from the talk, and it introduces the associated idea that the poetry readings are popular with college students.

Choice (D) uses the word *ten* from the talk and the idea that the readings are held weekly but it combines them in a way that is not true.

6. Who is John Taylor?

   (A) The owner of the Laughing Goat Cafe

   (B) A frequent participant at the poetry readings

   (C) The publisher of Contemporary Poetry magazine

   (D) A first-time participant at the poetry readings

Explanation: The correct answer is Choice (B). This is a Detail question. The speaker states this directly (*First up is one of our regulars, John Taylor.*) A "regular" is a person who goes somewhere or participates in an activity "regularly," meaning "frequently" or "often."

Choice (A) uses the cafe's name (*the Laughing Goat Cafe*) mentioned in the talk, but John Taylor is not identified as the cafe's owner.

Choice (C) uses the word *published* from the talk, and the title of one of the magazines mentioned (*Contemporary Poetry* magazine), but John Taylor is not the magazine's publisher.

Choice (D) rephrases *first-timers* from the talk, but John Taylor is not a first-time participant.

Practice 3

Narrator: *Questions 7 through 9 refer to the following talk.*

Man: *To help us keep better track of copier use, we're going to install a new Xcel 2000 photocopier, which is scheduled to arrive this weekend and will be ready for use on Monday. The new copier will have all the functions of the Xcel 1800 that we have now, but it will require you to enter a project authorization code, which you'll get from your project managers. So beginning next Monday, every time you need to make copies for a project you'll have to enter a code. You'll also be assigned a personal code, which you can use for general copying—but for work-related material, only, of course. The reason we're doing this is to try and reign in overhead costs. Some projects require enormous numbers of photocopies. For example, we photocopied almost 50,000 pages for the MetaWorks project. We're going to allow each project up to 5,000 pages free, and then we'll bill the client for each page over that. By using project authorization codes, we'll be able to track each project's page count accurately.*

7. When is a project code needed?

    (A) When ordering supplies
    (B) When filling out time sheets
    (C) When using the copy machine
    (D) When shipping packages overnight

Explanation: The correct answer is Choice (C). This is a Gist question. This question asks about the overall situation. It is made clear throughout the talk that the codes are required to use the photocopier.

Choices (A), (B), and (C) are not mentioned.

8. Who will give employees authorization codes?

    (A) MetaWorks
    (B) The speaker
    (C) Project managers
    (D) The human resources department

Explanation: The correct answer is Choice (C). This is a Detail question. The speaker says that employees will get the codes from project managers.

Choice (A) uses a name the speaker mentioned in the talk to illustrate the problem.

Choice (B) is not stated or implied.

Choice (D) is not mentioned.

9. When will employees begin using project codes?

    (A) Later that day

    (B) The next day

    (C) The following Monday

    (D) In two weeks

Explanation: The correct answer is Choice (C). This is a Detail question. This is stated directly (*So beginning next Monday, every time you need to make copies for a project you'll have to enter a code.*).

Choices (A), (B), and (D) are not mentioned.

Chapter 4:
Strategies for the TOEIC® Exam Reading Section

The Reading Section of the TOEIC exam has 3 Parts:

Part 5: Incomplete Sentences

Part 6: Text Completion

Part 7: Reading Comprehension

Each part has its own directions and strategies that will be discussed separately below.

Part 5: Incomplete Sentences

On the fifth part of the TOEIC exam, you will read a series of 40 sentences in your test book. Each sentence has a blank, marked with a dashed line (-------), where a word or phrase has been removed. Below each sentence are 4 answer choices. The answer choices are single words or short phrases that could fit into the blank to complete the sentence. You must select the answer choice that best completes the sentence.

The sentences are generally written in formal English as it is used in business and professional settings. The sentences reflect the kind of material you might read in a business report, a news story, an e-mail, a public notice, or in other everyday business contexts. The sentences can test either vocabulary or grammar.

(Because the sentences in Part 5 are not really "questions," they will be referred to as "items" in the text that follows.)

STRATEGY 1: KNOW THE DIRECTIONS

It is important to understand what you are being asked to do, and to be sure you know the directions before you take the test.

The directions for Part 5 will look like this:

READING TEST

In the Reading Section, you will read a variety of texts and answer different types of reading comprehension questions. The Reading Section will last 75 minutes. There are three parts, and directions are given for each part. You are encouraged to answer as many questions as possible within the allotted time.

Mark your answers on the separate answer sheet. Do not write them in the test book.

Part 5

Directions: A word or phrase is missing in the sentences below. Four answer choices are given below each of the sentences. Choose the best answer to complete the sentence. Then mark the letter on your answer sheet.

ETS does not provide an example sentence for Part 5. However, here is what a typical sentence looks like:

---

101. A late payment ------- of $25 will be applied to all accounts more than 30 days overdue.

   (A) fee
   (B) fare
   (C) cost
   (D) price

The sentence should read:

A late payment **fee** of $25 will be applied to all accounts more than 30 days overdue.

Therefore, you would mark (A) on your answer sheet.

Here is a second example:

---

102. Trillium Incorporated plans ------- branch offices in both Seoul and Pusan before the end of the year.

(A) open
(B) to open
(C) opened
(D) to be opened

The sentence should read:

Trillium Incorporated plans **to open** branch offices in both Seoul and Pusan before the end of the year.

Therefore, you would mark (B) on your answer sheet.

In the Listening Section, you must keep pace with the recording to avoid falling behind. If you answer a question quickly, you will still have to wait for the recording before continuing.

In the Reading Section, however, you must pace yourself: You have 75 minutes to complete all of Parts 5, 6, and 7. When you finish Part 5, you can immediately begin Part 6; when you have finished Part 6, you can immediately begin Part 7.

Part 5 begins with item 101 and ends with 140.

By knowing the Reading Section directions and the directions for Part 5 in advance, you can begin working on the Part 5 items immediately. You do not need to waste valuable time reading what you already know. As soon as you are told to begin the Reading Section, you should skip the directions and begin working on item number 101.

STRATEGY 2: DECIDE WHETHER THE SENTENCE TESTS VOCABULARY OR GRAMMAR

The sentences can be divided into 2 types of items, based on what the answer choices are:

Vocabulary items: *All the choices are from different word families but have similar meanings.*

In the first example sentence above, the answer choices are all nouns and are not part of the same word family. They do not share a common root, prefix, or suffix. Each word is different from the others in terms of its form. However, all of the words share a common theme: They are all related to money and payments. This is a classic example of a vocabulary item. To answer a vocabulary item, you must choose the word that completes the sentence *based on its meaning*. These items test the depth of your vocabulary.

Grammar items: *All the word choices are from the same word family.*

In the second example sentence above, the answer choices all contain the same word: *open.* This is a classic example of a grammar item. To answer a grammar item, you must choose the word that completes the sentence *based on its form*. These items test your command of grammar and structure.

(Note that vocabulary and grammar are not always so easily separated; some items may test vocabulary and grammar at the same time. Pronouns, comparatives, and other kinds of words can have different forms but still be related to each other. However, it is easiest to think in terms of 2 basic categories.)

The ways vocabulary and grammar items are approached are slightly different.

- For vocabulary items:

  Look for words and phrases that provide clues to the answer.

  Often, words or phrases in the sentence will help you eliminate distractors and point you toward the correct choice. In the first example above, the words "late" and "overdue" make choices *(B) fare, (C) cost,* and *(D) price* less attractive. *Fares, costs,* and *prices* are not usually "late" or "overdue."

- For grammar items:

  Focus on the words before and after the blank to determine which part of speech is required.

  Most often, the words immediately before and after the blank determine which part of speech the correct choice must be. Knowing this helps you to eliminate distractors. In the second example above, the word *plans* appears immediately before the blank must be followed by an infinitive, *to.* This eliminates choices *(A) open* and *(C) opened.*

STRATEGY 3: PREDICT THE ANSWER FOR EACH SENTENCE IN YOUR OWN WORDS BEFORE READING THE CHOICES

Read each sentence and try to fill the blank with your own word or phrase *before* reading the answer choices. If you understand the sentence, you should be able to correctly predict the word or phrase required to fill the blank. If your predicted answer is among the answer choices, this is likely to be the correct answer.

It is much better to have your own idea about the correct answer first, *before* looking at the answer choices. If you look at the answer choices first, you might be attracted to an incorrect choice.

STRATEGY 4: EVALUATE THE ANSWER CHOICES AND MARK THE ANSWER IF YOU KNOW IT

Find the answer choice that matches the answer you predicted. Before you mark your answer sheet, re-read the sentence to make sure the option you are choosing fills the blank the correctly.

If no answer choice matches your expected answer, eliminate as many choices as you can by doing the following:

- For vocabulary items, read the sentence for context clues that may point to the correct answer or help to eliminate distractors.

- For grammar items, focus on the words and phrases around the blank to determine the part of speech required, and eliminate distractors that do not fit.

After eliminating as many distractors as possible, select the best match from what is left.

If you cannot eliminate any distractors, choose one letter (A), (B), (C), or (D) and use this for every guessed answer. Using one letter consistently is better than guessing at random.

When you have decided on an answer choice, mark your answer sheet. Be sure to fill in the oval completely, as shown in the test directions.

STRATEGY 5: MANAGE YOUR TIME AND BE SURE TO ANSWER EVERY QUESTION

Time management is very important in the Reading Section. In the Listening Section, the timing is controlled by the audio recording. In the Reading Section, you have 75 minutes to complete Parts 5, 6, and 7. How quickly you move through each part is up to you. However, because Part 7—the last part of the test—is usually the most difficult and time-consuming, you will want to go through Parts 5 and 6 as quickly as you can so that you will have enough time left to finish Part 7.

Do not waste time working on any individual sentence. Although each sentence is worth the same amount, you should treat them all equally. Select your answer choice and mark it on your answer sheet as quickly as you can so that you can keep up with the test.

If you find yourself running out of time, mark your answer sheet with your "wild guess" letter (see **Strategy 7: Answer every question; choose one letter to use for all "wild guesses."** on page 15).

Do not leave any questions unanswered.

(N)

PART 5 STUDY TIPS

Vocabulary

The vocabulary tested on the TOEIC exam is the kind you would expect to see in business reports, newspaper or magazine articles, advertisements, public notices, and other types of everyday written contexts.

The best way to prepare yourself for Part 5 vocabulary items, obviously, is to increase your overall vocabulary; the best way to increase your vocabulary is to read as much authentic English material as you can. Read English-language newspapers and magazines on a regular basis. Many English-language newspapers and magazines are available free online; for example, you can read the *Washington Post* daily newspaper online at *www.washingtonpost.com.*

A good way to build your vocabulary is to write each new word you encounter in a notebook. Also write down the sentence that you found it in. Writing down new words helps you to remember them. You should also make note of new uses of words you already know and review your notebook often.

Grammar

The TOEIC exam tests a wide variety of grammar points. A full review of English grammar is beyond the scope of this book.

At a minimum, you should be familiar with the following:

Pronouns

- the uses of and differences among:
- possessive pronouns (mine, yours, his, hers, its, ours, theirs)
- subject pronouns (I, you, he, she, it, we, they)
- object pronouns (me, you, him, her, it, us, them)
- reflexive pronouns (myself, yourself, himself, herself, itself, ourselves, yourselves, themselves)
- relative pronouns (who, which, what, that)
- interrogative pronouns (who, which, what)
- demonstrative pronouns (this, that, these, those)

Verbs

- tenses and their usage
- when to use –*ing* forms
- infinitives with and without *to*
- common irregular verbs and their forms
- irregular past participles
- subject-verb agreement

Adjectives and Adverbs

- differences between adjectives and adverbs
- use of adjectives, including nouns as adjectives
- use and forms of comparatives and superlatives
- use of adverbs

Prepositions and Phrasal Verbs

- meaning and uses of common prepositions (*to, on, in, at, from ...*)

- meaning and uses of common prepositional phrases (*look up, go over, turn on ...*)

Conjunctions

- common conjunctions and their uses (*but, however, although, yet, so, despite ...*)

PART 5 STRATEGY SUMMARY

- Know the directions
- Decide whether the sentence tests vocabulary or grammar

For vocabulary items:

- Look for words and phrases that provide clues to the answer

For grammar items:

- Focus on the words before and after the blank to determine which part of speech is required

- Predict the answer for each sentence in your own words before reading the choices

- Evaluate the answer choices and mark the answer

- Manage your time and be sure to answer every question

PRACTICE QUESTIONS

Following are examples of the kinds of incomplete sentence items that you will find on the test. Answers and explanations begin on page 166.

Directions:

For each sentence, choose the word or phrase that best completes the sentence and mark your answer choice in the space provided.

Practice 1

Last Friday, Phaedra Industries ------- it was in merger talks with Tortoise Productions.

- (A) announced
- (B) announcer
- (C) announcing
- (D) announcement

Mark Your Answer:

Practice 2

We are still in the initial planning phase, identifying team members and ------- the scope of the project.

- (A) hiring
- (B) looking
- (C) refining
- (D) consenting

Mark Your Answer:

Practice 3

Tremmling Inc.'s fourth-quarter report, ------- was released to the public yesterday, shows that revenues are up 5.3 percent over the same period last year.

- (A) who
- (B) what
- (C) which
- (D) whose

Mark Your Answer:

Practice 4

One of the study's more surprising finds is that increased levels of atmospheric carbon dioxide may encourage many plant species to grow ------- than normal.

   (A) fast

   (B) faster

   (C) fastest

   (D) the fastest

Mark Your Answer: Ⓐ Ⓑ Ⓒ Ⓓ

Practice 5

As we discussed during your annual performance evaluation, your 7% salary ------- will be effective August 1.

   (A) pay

   (B) job

   (C) raise

   (D) vacation

Mark Your Answer: Ⓐ Ⓑ Ⓒ Ⓓ

Practice 6

Leather seating, power steering, passenger-side airbags, and air conditioning are all offered as optional -------.

- (A) cars
- (B) features
- (C) circumstances
- (D) accomplishments

Mark Your Answer:

ANSWERS AND EXPLANATIONS

Practice 1

Last Friday, Phaedra Industries ------- it was in merger talks with Tortoise Productions.

    (A) announced

    (B) announcer

    (C) announcing

    (D) announcement

Explanation: This is a grammar item. Each answer choice is a form of the word "announce." The correct answer is Choice (A).

By examining the words before and after the blank (*Phaedra Industries / it was*), it is clear that a verb in the past tense is required. Choice (B) is a noun. Choice (C) is an *–ing* form. Choice (D) is a noun.

Practice 2

We are still in the initial planning phase, identifying team members and ------- the scope of the project.

    (A) hiring

    (B) looking

    (C) refining

    (D) consenting

Explanation: This is a vocabulary item. None of the answer choices are in the same word family. The correct answer is Choice (C).

The words *planning phase* and the phrase *scope of the project* provide clues to the correct answer. *The scope of the project* is not something that can be hired, so choice (A) can be eliminated. Choice (B) is an attractive distractor, but to be correct it would require the preposition *at* to form the phrasal verb *looking at*. Choice (D) does not relate to the situation.

Practice 3

Tremmling Inc.'s fourth-quarter report, ------- was released to the public yesterday, shows that revenues are up 5.3 percent over the same period last year.

    (A) who
    (B) what
    (C) which
    (D) whose

Explanation: This looks like a vocabulary item, because all the choices seem to be separate, unrelated words. However, it is really more of a grammar item. All the choices are relative pronouns. The correct answer is Choice (C).

The subject of the sentence is the *fourth-quarter report*. Choice (A) uses the pronoun *who* to refer to Tremmling Inc., but this is incorrect; Tremmling was not released to the public. Choices (B) and (D) do not complete the sentence correctly.

Practice 4

One of the study's more surprising finds is that increased levels of atmospheric carbon dioxide may encourage many plant species to grow ------- than normal.

   (A) fast
   (B) faster
   (C) fastest
   (D) the fastest

Explanation: This is a grammar item testing the use of adjectives, comparatives, and superlatives. The correct answer is Choice (B). The words before and after the blank, (*grow / than normal*) provide clues to the correct answer. A comparative (*faster*) is usually followed by *than*. Choices (A), (C), and (D) do not fit the situation.

Practice 5

As we discussed during your annual performance evaluation, your 7% salary ------- will be effective August 1.

   (A) pay
   (B) job
   (C) raise
   (D) vacation

Explanation: This is a vocabulary item. None of the answer choices are in the same word family. The correct answer is Choice (C). The words are all related to jobs or work. The phrase *7% salary* provides a clue to the correct answer. Choice (A) *pay* is similar to the sentence word *salary*, but the resulting term *7 % salary pay* is incorrect. Similarly, when choices (B) and (D) are put into the sentence, the results are incorrect.

Practice 6

Leather seating, power steering, passenger-side airbags, and air conditioning are all offered as optional -------.

- (A) cars
- (B) features
- (C) circumstances
- (D) accomplishments

Explanation: This is a vocabulary item. None of the answer choices are in the same word family. The correct answer is Choice (B). The sentence describes items that can be added to a car at the time of purchase. Choice (A) refers to the general theme of the sentence, but is incorrect. Choices (C) and (D) do not relate to the situation.

Part 6: Text Completion

On the sixth part of the TOEIC exam, you will read a series of 4 short passages in your test book. Each passage has 3 sentences marked with a dashed line (-------), indicating that a word or phrase from the sentence has been removed. Below each sentence are 4 answer choices. The answer choices are single words or short phrases that could go into the blank to complete the sentence. You must select the answer choice that best completes the sentence.

The passages are typically short news articles, advertisements, public notices, memos, e-mail messages, letters, faxes and other business correspondence, instructions, and other kinds of everyday texts.

There are 4 sets of passages, each with 3 items, for a total of 12 items in Part 6. The items can test either vocabulary or grammar. A single sentence can be used to test two items, but this is rare.

Part 6 should look very familiar to you: Part 6 is simply Part 5, but with paragraphs instead of individual sentences. The strategies for tackling Part 6 items are nearly identical to those for Part 5.

The major difference between Part 5 and Part 6 items is that words or phrases in the blanks of some Part 6 items refer to information presented in other sentences. However, only a few of the items will do this. Most of the Part 6 items behave like Part 5 items: For the majority of Part 6 items, all the information you need is in the sentence with the blank.

The strategies for Part 6 are discussed on the following pages.

STRATEGY 1: KNOW THE DIRECTIONS

It is important to understand what you are being asked to do and to be sure you know the directions before you take the test.

The directions fo Part 6 will look like this:

Directions: Read the texts found in the following pages. A word or phrase is missing in the sentences below. Four answer choices are given below each of the sentences. Choose the best answer to complete the sentence. Then mark the letter on your answer sheet.

ETS does not provide an example for Part 6. However, here is what a typical Part 6 passage with 3 items looks like:

Questions 141–143 refer to the following course description.

Course Description:

Photography 120: Basic Photography for Everyone

Come to class prepared to have fun while learning to use your 35mm SLR film camera.

(Digital photography will NOT be covered in this class. See Course 121: *Basic Digital Imaging for Everyone*, or Course 122: *Turning Your Computer into a Digital Darkroom*.)

The course covers f-stops, shutter speeds, exposure, metering, film types, lenses, filters, flash photography, simple lighting techniques, composition and ways of "seeing," and hand-held and tripod shooting techniques.

There will be a different assignment each week. You will shoot both print and slide film, and work in color and black-and-white. You will be encouraged to share your photographs in class to receive feedback from your ------. To complete all the assignments you

141. (A) films
     (B) cameras
     (C) classmates
     (D) photographs

will ------ a minimum of 6 rolls of film. (The approximate

142. (A) shot
     (B) shoot
     (C) shoots
     (D) shooting

cost for film and processing is $85.)

Bring your 35 mm SLR camera to the first class, as well as your enthusiasm for learning a new skill. No experience necessary!

Required textbook: *Introduction to Photography, 2nd edition* by Don Hasbrook

(Note: A 35mm camera is the only equipment required for this class. If you do not own a ------, or have access

143. (A) car
     (B) camera
     (C) scanner
     (D) laptop computer

to one, you may rent one from the school for an additional fee. Subject to availability. Call the main office for details.)

STRATEGY 2: LOOK AT THE SENTENCES FOR THE INDIVIDUAL ITEMS FIRST: DECIDE WHETHER THEY TEST VOCABULARY OR GRAMMAR, AND WHETHER THEY REQUIRE INFORMATION FOUND IN OTHER PARTS OF THE PASSAGE

As stated earlier, the main difference between Part 5 and Part 6 is that some of the items in Part 6 need information that is found in other sentences in the passage. This means that, in addition to deciding whether an item tests vocabulary or grammar, you will need to determine *whether the item requires information from other parts of the passage*.

You may be tempted to read each Part 6 passage from beginning to end. However, because most of the items can be answered using only the information in the sentence containing the blank, you can use your time more effectively by focusing on reading only what you need to read to answer the items.

You should look at the item sentences first, to determine whether you can answer them without reading the rest of the passage. This will allow you to focus on reading only what you need to read to answer the items.

Look at the items in the example passage again.

Item 141: The answer choices are all nouns, and are not part of the same word family. The do not share a common root, prefix, or suffix. Each word is different from the others in terms of its form. This is a vocabulary item.

While the answer choices are all words associated with the theme of the passage, this item can be answered using only the information contained in the sentence containing the blank. It does not require reading any of the surrounding context. In this sense, it is really like a Part 5 vocabulary item.

Item 142: The answer choices are all forms of the word "shoot." This is a grammar item. Again, this item can be answered using only the information in the sentence containing the blank. None of the surrounding context is required. It is similar to a Part 5 grammar item.

Item 143: The answer choices are all nouns and are not part of the same word family. This is a vocabulary item. However, *each of the answer choices completes the sentence in a grammatical and logical way*. None of the answer choices can be eliminated based only on the item sentence itself. This kind of item is unlike the items found in Part 5. You will need to look at the surrounding context to determine which of the answer choices is consistent with the passage text.

Once you have determined whether an item tests vocabulary or grammar, you can follow the same steps that you did for Part 5:

- For vocabulary items:

    Look for words and phrases that provide clues to the answer.

    Often, words or phrases in the sentence will help you eliminate distractors and will point you toward the correct choice. In item 141 from the example above, the phrase "to receive feedback from" makes choices *(A) films*, *(B) cameras*, and *(D) photographs* less attractive. *Films*, *camera*, and *photographs* cannot provide feedback.

- For grammar items:

    Focus on the words before and after the blank to determine which part of speech is required.

    Most often, the words immediately before and after the blank determine which part of speech the correct choice must be. Knowing this helps you to eliminate distractors.

In item 142 from the example above, the words "you will" immediately before the blank must be followed by an infinitive, *to*. This eliminates choices *(A) shot*, *(C) shoots*, and *(D) shooting*.

If the item can be answered using only the information in the sentence containing the blank, you should go ahead and answer it.

For items that require information from other parts of the passage, first look at the sentences that come earlier. The information you need will most often be found near the sentence containing the blank, usually one or two sentences before it. If you do not find the information you need there, look one or two sentences past the sentence containing the blank. If you still cannot find the information, try reading the passage from the beginning. Usually, you will not need to do this.

STRATEGY 3: PREDICT THE ANSWER FOR EACH ITEM IN YOUR OWN WORDS BEFORE READING THE CHOICES

Just as you did for Part 5, read each item and try to fill the blank with your own word or phrase *before* reading the answer choices. Because many of the items do not actually require the surrounding passage text, you will often be able to read the item sentence by itself and correctly predict the word or phrase required to fill the blank. If your predicted answer is among the answer choices, this is likely to be the correct answer.

It is much better to have your own idea about the correct answer first, *before* looking at the answer choices. If you look at the answer choices first, you might be attracted to an incorrect choice.

STRATEGY 4: EVALUATE THE ANSWER CHOICES AND MARK THE ANSWER

Find the answer choice that matches the answer you predicted. Before you mark your answer sheet, re-read the sentence to make sure the option you are choosing fills the blank the correctly.

If no answer choice matches your expected answer, eliminate as many choices as you can by doing the following:

- For vocabulary items, read the sentence for context clues that may point to the correct answer or help to eliminate distractors.

- For grammar items, focus on the words and phrases around the blank to determine the part of speech required and eliminate distractors that do not fit.

- Look at the sentences around the sentence containing the blank to see if there is any additional information you can use.

After eliminating as many distractors as possible, select the best match from what is left.

If you cannot eliminate any distractors, choose one letter (A), (B), (C), or (D) and use this for every guessed answer. Using one letter consistently is better than guessing at random.

When you have decided on an answer choice, mark your answer sheet. Be sure to fill in the oval completely, as shown in the test directions.

STRATEGY 5: MANAGE YOUR TIME AND BE SURE TO ANSWER EVERY QUESTION

Time management is very important in the Reading Section. In the Listening Section, the timing is controlled by the audio recording. In the Reading Section, you have 75 minutes to complete Parts 5, 6, and 7. How quickly you move through each part is up to you. Part 7—the last part of the test—is usually the most difficult and time-consuming, so you will want to go through Part 6 as quickly as you can so you will have enough time left to finish Part 7.

By determining whether you can answer an item using only the information in the sentence (see Strategy 2), you should be able to avoid reading too much, which will save you time.

Do not waste time working on any individual item. Although each item is worth the same amount, you should treat them all equally. You must not allow yourself to fall behind by spending too much time with any one item. Select your answer choice and mark it on your answer sheet as quickly as you can so that you can keep up with the test.

If you find yourself running out of time, mark your answer sheet with your "wild guess" letter (see **Strategy 7: Answer every question; choose one letter to use for all "wild guesses."** on page 15).

Do not leave any questions unanswered.

PART 6 STRATEGY SUMMARY

- Know the directions
- Look at the sentences for the individual items first: Decide whether they test vocabulary or grammar, and whether they require information found in other parts of the passage

   For vocabulary items:

   - Look for words and phrases that provide clues to the answer

   For grammar items:

   - Focus on the words before and after the blank to determine which part of speech is required

   - For items that require information from other parts of the passage, first look for the information in the sentences that comes immediately *before* the sentence containing the blank.

- Predict the answer for each sentence in your own words before reading the choices
- Evaluate the answer choices and mark the answer
- Manage your time and be sure to answer every question

PRACTICE QUESTIONS

Following are examples of the kinds of text completion items that you will find on the TOEIC exam. Answers and explanations begin on page 183.

Directions: Read the texts found in the following pages. A word or phrase is missing in the sentences below. Four answer choices are given below each of the sentences. Choose the best answer to complete the sentence. Then mark the letter on your answer sheet.

Practice 1

Questions 144–146 refer to the following article.

MORE AMERICAN HOUSEHOLDS BANKING ONLINE

The number of American households doing their banking online grew by 39.2 percent last year. Experts predict that number to increase by a ------- 22.5 percent this year, and

144. (A) more
     (B) larger
     (C) further
     (D) superior

another 17.6 percent the year after. A total of 33.2 million American households are currently banking online. Young adults ages 24 to 35 with household incomes of $75,000 or higher are most likely to do their banking online. Today, nearly ------- that group (48 percent) views

145. (A) half
     (B) twice
     (C) double
     (D) two times

bills online, and 46 percent pays bills online. Older adults, those over 65, at all income levels, are the least likely to bank online.

A representative for the American Association of Online Bankers says banks ------- their customers to bank online,

146. (A) to encourage
     (B) encouragement
     (C) are encouraging
     (D) have been encouraged

"because online banking is much cheaper for banks to provide than traditional in-person teller services."

Practice 2

Questions 147–149 refer to the following memorandum.

MEMORANDUM

To: All TigerNet employees
From: John Sullivan, CEO
Date: April 4th, 20 –
Subject: Our Future

The recent collapse of our biggest competitor has many of you wondering whether the same thing could happen here. I would like to set the record straight.

Today, TigerNet is positioned for -------. We are the

147. (A) success
(B) pleasure
(C) collapse
(D) disappointment

market leader with the highest quality, most functionally complete products and proven technology, the strongest balance sheet and financial viability, the most experienced and dedicated workforce, and the most tried, tested, and proven management team in the industry.

While the severe current conditions have weakened many of our competitors—dozens of Internet service providers both small and large have ------- from the marketplace—

148. (A) isolated
(B) decreased
(C) withdrawn
(D) consolidated

we are increasing our market share. As the market continues to consolidate, TigerNet will actually grow.

We see enormous business opportunities ahead, and expect ------- to thrive for at least the next several years.

149. (A) the company
(B) a balance sheet
(C) our competitors
(D) their market share

Our future is bright.
-JS-

Practice 3

Questions 150–152 refer to the following instructions.

TROUBLESHOOTING YOUR DSL MODEM

Most connection problems ------ by trying one of the following.

150. (A) does solve
     (B) are solving
     (C) could solve
     (D) can be solved

1. Power cycle—Shut off both the modem and the
   computer and wait for 30 seconds. Turn the modem
   back on first, and then turn on the computer. After
   the PPPoE light stops blinking and stays on, you can
   reconnect to the Internet. NOTE: If your modem does
   not have an on/off switch, ------- the modem

151. (A) insert
     (B) depart
     (C) unplug
     (D) enclose

from the electrical wall outlet to turn it off.

2. Check for line interference—Make sure your modem is
   not on or ------- other electrical devices that may

152. (A) in
     (B) off
     (C) near
     (D) throughout

interfere with the signal. This includes your computer
monitor, stereo speakers, cordless phone (or its base),
or a halogen light.

3. Call the Peacelink Telephone Support Center—You
   can talk to a technical support representative. Hours of
   operation are Monday through Friday, 7:00 AM to midnight, Eastern time, and Saturday and Sunday 9:00 AM
   to 10:00 PM Eastern. 1-800-555-HELP.

ANSWERS AND EXPLANATIONS

Practice 1

Questions 144–146 refer to the following article.

MORE AMERICAN HOUSEHOLDS BANKING ONLINE

The number of American households doing their banking online grew by 39.2 percent last year. Experts predict that number to increase by a ------- 22.5 percent this year, and

144. (A) more
     (B) larger
     (C) further
     (D) superior

another 17.6 percent the year after. A total of 33.2 million American households are currently banking online. Young adults ages 24 to 35 with household incomes of $75,000 or higher are most likely to do their banking online. Today, nearly ------- that group (48 percent) views

145. (A) half
     (B) twice
     (C) double
     (D) two times

bills online, and 46 percent pays bills online. Older adults, those over 65, at all income levels, are the least likely to bank online.

A representative for the American Association of Online Bankers says banks ------- their customers to bank online,

146. (A) to encourage
     (B) encouragement
     (C) are encouraging
     (D) have been encouraged

"because online banking is much cheaper for banks to provide than traditional in-person teller services."

Explanation:

144. This is a vocabulary item. The choices are all adjectives. The item can be answered using the information in the sentence containing the blank. The correct Choice is (C). The choices are all related in meaning, but only (C) completes the sentence correctly.

145. This is primarily a vocabulary item, but it has elements of grammar in it. The choices are all separate words related to the number two. The item can be answered using the information in the sentence containing the blank. The correct Choice is (A). The choices are all related in meaning and can complete the sentence grammatically, but only (A) completes the sentence logically. Forty-eight percent is "nearly half."

146. This is a grammar item. The choices are all forms of the word "encourage." The item can be answered using the information in the sentence containing the blank. The correct Choice is (C). The words around the blank indicate the tense should be present, present continuous, or present perfect. Choice (C) is in the present continuous.

Practice 2

Questions 147–149 refer to the following memorandum.

MEMORANDUM

To: All TigerNet employees
From: John Sullivan, CEO
Date: April 4th, 20 –
Subject: Our Future

The recent collapse of our biggest competitor has many of you wondering whether the same thing could happen here. I would like to set the record straight.

Today, TigerNet is positioned for -------. We are the

147. (A) success
     (B) pleasure
     (C) collapse
     (D) disappointment

market leader with the highest quality, most functionally complete products and proven technology, the strongest balance sheet and financial viability, the most experienced and dedicated workforce, and the most tried, tested, and proven management team in the industry.

While the severe current conditions have weakened many of our competitors—dozens of Internet service providers both small and large have ------- from the marketplace—

148. (A) isolated
     (B) decreased
     (C) withdrawn
     (D) consolidated

we are increasing our market share. As the market continues to consolidate, TigerNet will actually grow.

We see enormous business opportunities ahead, and expect ------- to thrive for at least the next several years.

149. (A) the company
     (B) a balance sheet
     (C) our competitors
     (D) their market share

Our future is bright.
-JS-

Explanation:

147. This is a vocabulary item. The choices are all nouns. The answer choices all complete the sentence grammatically, so information from other parts of the passage is needed. The correct Choice is (A). This is a case where the additional information comes *after* the sentence. The passage goes on to describe the company's future as being positive. Choices (C) and (D) are negative. Choice (B) fits grammatically but sounds awkward and is not logical.

148. This is a vocabulary item, but it has elements of grammar in it. The choices are all verbs. The item can be answered using the information in the sentence containing the blank. The correct answer is Choice (C). Although the item deals mainly with vocabulary, the phrase "from the market place" immediately after the blank limits the choices. Only (C) completes the sentence correctly.

149. This is a vocabulary item, but it has elements of grammar in it. The choices are all nouns or noun phrases, but only (A) and (C) make logical and grammatical sense. Some help from the surrounding context is required to eliminate (C). Clearly the focus is on the company thriving, not the company's competitors. The correct answer is Choice (A).

Practice 3

Questions 150–152 refer to the following instructions.

TROUBLESHOOTING YOUR DSL MODEM

Most connection problems ------ by trying one of the following.

150. (A) does solve
    (B) are solving
    (C) could solve
    (D) can be solved

1. Power cycle—Shut off both the modem and the computer and wait for 30 seconds. Turn the modem back on first, and then turn on the computer. After the PPPoE light stops blinking and stays on, you can reconnect to the Internet. NOTE: If your modem does not have an on/off switch, ------- the modem

151. (A) insert
    (B) depart
    (C) unplug
    (D) enclose

from the electrical wall outlet to turn it off.

2. Check for line interference—Make sure your modem is not on or ------- other electrical devices that may

152. (A) in
    (B) off
    (C) near
    (D) throughout

interfere with the signal. This includes your computer monitor, stereo speakers, cordless phone (or its base), or a halogen light.

3. Call the Peacelink Telephone Support Center—You can talk to a technical support representative. Hours of operation are Monday through Friday, 7:00 AM to midnight, Eastern time, and Saturday and Sunday 9:00 AM to 10:00 PM Eastern. 1-800-555-HELP.

Explanation:

150. This is a grammar item. The choices are all forms of the word "solve." The item can be answered using the information in the sentence containing the blank. The correct answer is Choice (D). The other choices do not complete the sentence grammatically.

151. This is a vocabulary item. The choices are all verbs. The item can be answered using the information in the sentence containing the blank. The correct answer is Choice (C). Only (C) completes the sentence correctly.

152. This is a vocabulary item. The choices are all prepositions. The item can be answered using the information in the sentence containing the blank. The correct answer is Choice (C). Only choice (C) completes the sentence correctly.

Part 7: Reading Comprehension

In Part 7 of the TOEIC exam, you will read a series of short passages in your test book. Each passage is followed by 2 to 5 questions. Each question has 4 answer choices. You must select the answer choice that best answers the question and mark it on your answer sheet.

Part 7 begins with question 153 and ends with question 200. There are a total of 48 questions in Part 7.

There are two kinds of reading passages in Part 7:

1. **Single Passage:** one reading passage, followed by 2 to 5 questions. There are usually 9 single-item passages. These are questions 153–184. Single passages make up more than half of Part 7 (28 of 48 questions).

2. **Double Passages:** a set of two related reading passages, always followed by 5 questions. There are 4 sets of double passages. These are the last passages in Part 7, questions 185-200.

The passages are typically short news articles, advertisements, public notices, memos, e-mail messages, letters, faxes and other business correspondence, instructions, and other kinds of everyday texts. They also include graphs, charts, tables, schedules, and other information of this kind.

The questions typically ask about details provided in the passage; inferences that can be made based on the information presented; and about the meaning of words as they are used in the passage. The questions generally ask about information in the order that it is presented in the passage.

For the double passages, there is usually at least one question requiring you to use information found in both passages.

STRATEGY 1: KNOW THE DIRECTIONS

It is important to understand what you are being asked to do, and to be sure you know the directions before taking the test.

The directions for Part 7 will look like this:

> **Directions:** In this part, you will read a selection of text, such as magazine or newspaper articles, letters or advertisements. Each text is followed by several questions. Select the best answer for each question and mark the letter on your answer sheet.

Here is an example of a Part 7 single passage:

Questions 153–155 refer to the following article.

Low Crop Prices Hurt Farmers

Unusually low prices for crops are causing hardships for farmers in Canada. Together with a strong Canadian dollar and rising costs, this has led to large-scale losses on many Canadian farms. The Canadian government forecasts net farm income (NFI) this year at $870 million, a significant decline from last year's $1.8 billion NFI.

NFI for the province of Saskatchewan is again likely to be negative this year at an estimated minus $207 million, compared with minus $77 million last year.

Manitoba, which is still recovering from floods earlier in the year, is also expected to fall behind expenses and is forecast to have an NFI deficit of $195 million.

Alberta, with its large-scale cattle industry, is generating more income than provinces where farming is based on grains. This year's NFI is forecast at $258 million.

Even at the current low prices, farmers in Saskatchewan and Manitoba are having a hard time selling their grains, due to this year's below-average quality harvest.

Elsewhere, good returns on dairy, eggs, fruit, and poultry have boosted farm incomes.

---

153. What is expected for net farm income in Canada?

    (A) It will be much lower than the year before.

    (B) It will be about the same as the year before.

    (C) It will be higher than original government forecasts.

    (D) It will be significantly lower than the original government forecasts.

154. According to the article, which Canadian farm product is selling poorly?

    (A) Nuts

    (B) Fruit

    (C) Dairy

    (D) Grains

155. Which of the following is NOT mentioned as a problem Canadian farmers are facing?

    (A) Floods

    (B) Rising costs

    (C) Low cattle prices

    (D) Poor quality crops

Here is an example of a Part 7 double passage.

Questions 181–185 refer to the following advertisement and registration form.

Revolutionize your investment strategies in as little as one hour!
Thursday, February 12 at 7:00 PM
Carlton Hotel, St. Morton, LA

We would like to invite you to join renowned investment expert Sandra Gellert for an exclusive free investment seminar.

Sandra is Chief Investment Officer and Portfolio Manager of ALC Investments. She recognizes the strong economic environment in Louisiana right now and would like to help YOU with your investment strategy.

Three-time recipient of the coveted national Fund Manager of the Year award, Sandra brings vision as well as everyday good sense to strategic financial planning. She holds a Bachelor of Commerce degree, a Master of Business Administration degree, a Doctorate in Finance, and is a Chartered Financial Analyst. This education combined with a wealth of successful experience in managing financial portfolios means this seminar is an exciting opportunity for disciplined investment planning.

Topics to be covered:
   Wealth Creation
   Global Investment
   Financial Services
   Oil and Gas
   Pensions and Retirement Funds
   Foreign Exchange Markets
   Specific Company Suggestions

Seating at this event is limited. Please register for this exclusive free session online, or fill out the registration form on the back of this flyer and fax it to the number given below.

Register Online: *www.alcinvestments.com/seminar/registration.html*
Register by Fax: 456-223-1232

This seminar with Sandra Gellert, one of the nation's most sought-after speakers on investments, is sponsored by Synergy Financial, St. Morton City Bank, and Integrated Wealth Services Inc.

(Registration form on back)

REGISTRATION FORM

An Evening with Sandra Gellert
Thursday, February 12
Carlton Hotel in St. Morton, LA 7:00 PM
Limited Spaces - Register Now!

Name: <u>Paolo Grazzi</u>

Company: <u>Consolidated Investments</u>

Position in Organization: <u>Senior Financial Advisor</u>

Address: <u>125 67th Street, St. Morton, LA</u>

Tel (work): <u>456-852-1386</u>

Tel (evening): <u>456-852-7221</u>

email: <u>paolog@consolidatedinvestments.com</u>

No. of participants (max 3 per registration): <u>2</u>

Name of additional participant: <u>Michelle Dubois</u>

Name of additional participant: <u>N/A</u>

Special interests: <u>International investments, oil and gas,</u>
<u>retirement funds</u>

---

181. What is learned about Sandra Gellert?

   (A) She has taught at several universities.

   (B) She has won an award for her latest book.

   (C) She has several business-related degrees.

   (D) She has over 20 years' experience in the
       financial field.

182. Which of the following will NOT be discussed by Sandra Gellert?

(A) Real estate

(B) Currency trading

(C) Retirement planning

(D) Investing internationally

183. Who is said to be one of the seminar's sponsors?

(A) Michelle Dubois

(B) Consolidated Investments

(C) The Morton Chamber of Commerce

(D) Integrated Wealth Services Inc.

184. What is learned about Paolo Grazzi?

(A) He has charged the registration to a credit card.

(B) He is especially interested in technology stocks.

(C) He will attend the presentation with one other person.

(D) He is the Chief Investment Officer for Consolidated Investments.

185. What will Paolo Grazzi probably do?

(A) Fax his registration card

(B) Meet Sandra Gellert for lunch

(C) Go directly to the Carlton Hotel from the airport

(D) Discuss his investment strategy with Michelle Dubois

STRATEGY 2: UNDERSTAND QUESTION TYPES AND HOW QUESTIONS ARE ORDERED

The questions usually ask for information in the order it is presented in the passage. For example, for a 3-question passage, the first question will usually ask about information found near the beginning, the second question will ask about something found in the middle, and the third question will ask about something mentioned near the end.

There are four basic categories of questions for Part 7:

1. **Gist**

    Gist questions will ask what the main topic is, why the passage has been written, or what the passage's purpose is. Gist questions ask about the overall situation, rather than about specific details.

    Following are examples of gist questions:

    > What is the article mainly about?

    > Why has the bank written this letter?

    > What is the main purpose of this e-mail?

    > What is learned about the company?

    There is usually one gist question per passage.

2. **Detail**

    Detail questions ask about information mentioned in the passage. They can ask about general information, or very specific details. Examples of what detail questions might ask about include what products or services a company provides; how much a product or service costs; when or where an action or event will take place; what role, function, or responsibility people will have; how a problem or situation is being handled; the order or manner in which things are to be done.

Following are examples of detail questions:

What service does Miller Consulting provide?

How much are the XJ100s?

Where will the meeting be held?

When is the report due?

What will Rob Dollison be responsible for doing?

How should the filter be cared for?

Some detail questions are asked using NOT. For example:

What is NOT a service provided by Miller Consulting?

What is NOT included on the meeting agenda?

Which of the following is NOT on sale?

Why will the goods NOT be shipped that day?

For these questions, you must read the choices carefully. For the first example (*What is NOT a service provided by Miller Consulting?*), three of the four options will be services that ARE provided. You need to pick the one that is NOT provided. Be careful!

Detail questions are the most common Part 7 questions. There is often more than one per passage.

3. **Implication/Inference**

Implication/inference questions ask about things that are not stated directly in the passage. They often require you to make connections between information that has been presented in different parts of the passage. They may ask about expectations, possibilities, or probable future actions; they can refer to people's emotions or feelings.

The following are examples of implication/inference questions:

> Why were analysts surprised by the earnings announcement?
>
> What does Mr. Davis imply about the price of his products?
>
> Why does Mrs. Lopez mention April 10th in her e-mail?
>
> What can be inferred about Tezla Corp.'s annual budget?

There is usually one implication/inference question per passage.

At times, Implication/Inference questions and Gist questions may seem to be similar. For example, a Gist question that asks about the purpose of an e-mail message might require drawing an inference; the message might provide enough information to make the purpose obvious, but that information might not be stated directly in the e-mail.

Although some Gist questions require you to understand an implication or make an inference, their focus is on the larger picture or the overall situation. Implication/Inference questions tend to deal with implied details about the situation or context itself.

4. **Vocabulary**

Vocabulary questions ask you to identify the meaning of a word as it is used in the passage. They will refer to a specific line in a paragraph and will always have the same format.

For example:

The word "coveted" in paragraph 2, line 4, is closest in meaning to

(A) devoted
(B) desirable
(C) fashionable
(D) advantageous

Vocabulary questions are not very common. There are usually no more than 3 on the entire test. They are usually found in the 4-question and 5-question passages and are usually the last questions in the set.

STRATEGY 3: UNDERSTAND THE BASIC TYPES OF DISTRACTORS

To understand the kinds of Part 7 distractors and how they work, you first need to understand how ETS writes test items.

All Part 7 distractors must answer the question "plausibly," that is, they must be possible answers to the question. When you read a Part 7 question and the answer choices by themselves—without referring to the reading passage—each choice will answer the question in a logical and realistic way, and no choice can be eliminated using logic or common sense. Each option will be a plausible answer to the question. There are no "impossible" answer choices. All Part 7 items are written in this way.

Note that none of the Part 7 questions are "linked" in any way, that is, the information contained in a set of question and answer choices will not help you to answer any other questions.

Following is an example:

What is enclosed with the letter?

(A) A coupon
(B) A payment
(C) An invoice
(D) A brochure

The following are the basic types of distractors for Part 7 items:

1. **Not Mentioned**

   This type of distractor refers to things or ideas commonly associated with the passage content but which are not actually mentioned in the passage. The distractor answers the question plausibly but it does not relate to the actual passage content.

2. **Repeated Words**

   This type of distractor uses a key word or phrase from the passage, but it is not true. The distractor answers the question plausibly but is incorrect.

3. **Incorrect Paraphrase/Misstatement**

   This type of distractor uses specific language, facts, or ideas that are mentioned or implied in the passage, but it rephrases, paraphrases, and twists them so that they are not true. The distractor often contradicts or misstates the facts. Sometimes important information is omitted or new information is added. Most of the content of the distractor comes directly from the passage. The distractor answers the question plausibly but it is incorrect.

   (Incorrect choices for Vocabulary questions can all be considered "incorrect paraphrase/misstatement" distractors because they incorrectly paraphrase they vocabulary word being tested.)

KAPLAN

4. **Hybrid**

This is not actually a basic distractor type; it is a combination of two or more of the three basic types outlined above.

A set of answer choices may use more than one type of distractor at a time.

Each distractor type is discussed separately on the following pages.

Look at the Part 7 single passage example again.

Questions 153–155 refer to the following article.

Low Crop Prices Hurt Farmers

Unusually low prices for crops are causing hardships for farmers in Canada. Together with a strong Canadian dollar and rising costs, this has led to large-scale losses on many Canadian farms. The Canadian government forecasts net farm income (NFI) this year at $870 million, a significant decline from last year's $1.8 billion NFI.

NFI for the province of Saskatchewan is again likely to be negative this year at an estimated minus $207 million, compared with minus $77 million last year.

Manitoba, which is still recovering from floods earlier in the year, is also expected to fall behind expenses and is forecast to have an NFI deficit of $195 million.

Alberta, with its large-scale cattle industry, is generating more income than provinces where farming is based on grains. This year's NFI is forecast at $258 million.

Even at the current low prices, farmers in Saskatchewan and Manitoba are having a hard time selling their grains, due to this year's below-average quality harvest.

Elsewhere, good returns on dairy, eggs, fruit, and poultry have boosted farm incomes.

---

153. What is expected for net farm income in Canada?

    (A) It will be much lower than the year before.
    (B) It will be about the same as the year before.
    (C) It will be higher than original government forecasts.
    (D) It will be significantly lower than the original government forecasts.

This is a Detail question. The correct answer is Choice (A).

Choice (B) misstates the information presented in the first paragraph. This is an example of an "incorrect paraphrase/misstatement" distractor.

Choice (C) contradicts the information in the first paragraph. This is an example of an "incorrect paraphrase/ misstatement" distractor.

Choice (D) repeats the words *significantly* and *government forecasts* from the first paragraph but it twists the facts. It also refers to an "original" forecast that was not mentioned. This is an example of a "hybrid" distractor.

---

154. According to the article, which Canadian farm product is selling poorly?

    (A) Nuts
    (B) Fruit
    (C) Dairy
    (D) Grains

This is a Detail question. The correct answer is Choice (D).

KAPLAN

Choice (A) is not mentioned in the passage. This is an example of a "not mentioned" distractor.

Choices (B), and (C) are both words mentioned in the passage, but they are incorrect. These are examples of "repeated words" distractors.

---

155. Which of the following is NOT mentioned as a problem Canadian farmers are facing?

    (A) Floods
    (B) Rising costs
    (C) Low cattle prices
    (D) Poor quality crops

This is a Detail question using the NOT format. The correct answer is Choice (C).

Choices (A), (B), and (D) are all mentioned as being problems for Canadian farmers.

Notice that for each of the questions, all the distractors are plausible answers and that none of the questions or answer choices are of any help in answering other questions.

STRATEGY 4: KNOW HOW TO READ PASSAGES

Because you have a limited amount of time to read the passages and answer the questions, you must be an efficient reader. Reading every word of every passage is not reading efficiently. Efficient reading requires *skimming* and *scanning*, described below.

Skim the passage to understand its overall contents

Skimming a passage means reading it quickly to understand the main points. When you skim a passage, you are interested in identifying the main idea or main topic. Your goal is to answer the question "What is this passage mainly about?"

For the example passage above, the answer to the question *"What is the passage mainly about?"* would be something like: Income from farming in Canada.

For the double passage example above, the answer to the question *"What are the passages mainly about?"* would be something like: An upcoming investment seminar and the details of someone's registration for the seminar.

To skim a passage, begin at the top of the passage and read only the first few words of each sentence. This should be enough to give you a sense of what the passage is about. Look for and make note of words or phrases that are repeated throughout the passage— these are probably important.

You do not need to read every word of the passage to find the main idea. You are not interested in details—yet.

Read the questions to find out what information is needed

The passages contain more information than you need to answer the questions; there are things mentioned in the passage that are not tested.

Your goal is *not* to read the entire passage. Your goal is only to answer the questions. The most efficient way to do this is to know what it is you are looking for *before* you read the passage in depth.

Read the questions—but not the answer choices—so that you will know what information you will need to find when you read the passage.

Answer each question in your own words before reading the choices

Read each question and predict the answer in your own words *before* reading the answer choices. If you understand the passage, you should be able to answer the questions in your own words. For each question, your predicted answer—or one very closely matching your predicted answer—should be among the answer choices.

Remember, there are no "trick" questions on the TOEIC exam. All the information needed to answer the questions is presented in the passage.

If you read the answer choices first—without answering the question in your own words—you are allowing the ETS test writers to put ideas into your head. You will be tempted to make the answer one of the distractors. It is much better to have your own idea about the correct answer first, *before* looking at the ETS answer choices.

Scan the passage to locate the material you need

Once you know what information you need to find, you should *scan* the passage to find it. *Scanning* is the process of looking for the key words and phrases you need to answer the questions.

Because you have read the questions and know what information to look for, you do not need to read every word in the passage. You only need to find the key words from the questions.

To scan a passage, start at the top and let your eyes go back and forth across the page; look for key words and phrases as you make your way to the bottom of the passage. You are looking only for the answers to the questions.

STRATEGY 5: EVALUATE THE ANSWER CHOICES AND MARK THE ANSWER IF YOU KNOW IT

After you have scanned the passage to find the information you need, you will need to evaluate the answer choices.

Find the answer choice that is the closest match to the answer you have been expecting and mark your answer sheet. Be sure to fill in the oval completely, as shown in the directions.

If none of the choices match your expected answer very well, you must eliminate as many choices as you can. Remember, because one question and answer choice set will not help you answer another; do not look at answer choices from one question for clues to answer another question.

STRATEGY 6: ELIMINATE ANSWER CHOICES THAT ARE WRONG AND SELECT THE BEST MATCH FROM WHAT IS LEFT

What if none of the answer choices match your expected answer very well? You must eliminate as many wrong choices as you can.

If you must guess, eliminate any choices that do not use words and phrases from the passage—the "not mentioned" distracter type. The "not mentioned" distractors are often the easiest to eliminate.

If only one of the answer choices use words and phrases that you recognize from the passage, this is likely to be the correct one.

STRATEGY 7: CONSIDER TACKLING THE SHORTER PASSAGES AND VOCABULARY QUESTIONS FIRST

This strategy is not for everyone. If you are the kind of person who is nervous about "breaking the rules," go ahead and answer the questions in the order in which they occur in your test book. There are some risks in tackling the shorter passages first, which will be explained below.

In the Listening Section, the order of the questions is controlled by the audio. In the Reading section, you are free to answer the questions in any order you choose. There is no rule that says you have to go through the passages in the order in which they are printed in your test book. ETS would prefer that you answer the questions in the order they appear, but this does not mean you cannot answer them in another order.

The reading passages have between 2 and 5 questions each. Generally, passages with fewer questions are shorter and easier than passages with more questions. Therefore, you might consider tackling the short passages first.

The advantage to this approach is that you will probably answer more questions in a shorter amount of time, and more questions answered means a potentially higher score. If you answer the questions in the order they are presented, you may be slowed down by harder questions and run out of time, leaving easier questions you might have been able to answer unanswered. If you answer all the easy questions first, you are that much closer to being finished, and you can use your remaining time to work on the more difficult passages.

The basic idea is to answer all the 2-question passages first, then the 3-question passages, then the 4-question passages, and so on.

Some of the reading passages will have a question that asks about how a particular word is used in the passage. These are generally easy questions, and you should try to answer them first. If you are running out of time, look for these questions, scan the passage to find the word, and try to answer the question. Often, if you know the word being tested, you can eliminate one or two answer choices without even reading the passage.

The major disadvantage of answering the questions out of order is that you risk making careless mistakes on your answer sheet—marking the wrong oval or even missing an entire passage. If you make such a mistake, you could wind up with a lower score.

If you decide to answer the questions out of order, make absolutely sure you are marking your answer sheet correctly. Double-check to be sure you have not accidentally filled in the wrong oval on your answer sheet. When the end of the test is near, check your answer sheet again to make sure you have not skipped any questions.

If you are careful not to make mistakes, this strategy can be very effective.

STRATEGY 8: IF YOU FINISH EARLY, GO BACK AND CHECK YOUR WORK FOR MISTAKES

Everyone makes mistakes, especially when under pressure. If you finish the test before time is called, you should check your answer sheet to make sure you have not missed any questions or marked your answer sheet incorrectly in any way. Check your work for Parts 5 and 6, as well.

STRATEGY 9: IF YOU FIND YOURSELF RUNNING OUT OF TIME, MARK YOUR ANSWER SHEET WITH YOUR "WILD GUESS" LETTER

Do not leave any questions unanswered.

(See *Strategy 7: Answer every question; choose one letter to use for all "wild guesses."* on page 13).

PART 7 STRATEGY SUMMARY

- Know the directions

- Understand question types and how questions are ordered

- Understand the basic types of distractors

- Know how to read passages

- Evaluate the answer choices and mark the answer if you know it

- Eliminate answer choices that are wrong and select the best match from what is left

- Consider tackling the shorter passages and vocabulary questions first

- If you finish early, go back and check your work for mistakes

- If you find yourself running out of time, mark your answer sheet with your "wild guess" letter

PRACTICE QUESTIONS

Directions

Read the passages and answer the questions. Mark your answers in the space provided.

Practice 1

Questions 156–158 refer to the following article.

State Approves $2.5 billion Solar Subsidy

California regulators have approved a $2.5 billion subsidy package for solar power. The subsidy program is the largest ever in the United States and promises more business for solar panel manufacturers such as SunTastic and SolarWatt who are already struggling to meet current levels of demand.

The state plans to hand out the money over the next 10 years in the form of rebates for consumers and businesses that install solar power facilities. It will probably be several years before manufacturers can meet rising demand for solar panels. Producers in Germany and other European countries also have backlogs of orders.

Global production of solar panels grew 37 percent last year, according to figures provided by the consulting firm Solar Tech Research, and manufacturers everywhere are selling all they can produce. Supporters of the California subsidy say it will encourage manufacturers to add the necessary capacity to meet the demand. Opponents suggest that the move may only serve to keep prices high.

Dr. Sergei Balakirev, director of the Energy Institute at the California Technical College, says that the price of solar power is still too high, which discourages most people from adopting the technology. A typical residential system costs $24,000 to install and yields electricity costing about 26 cents per kilowatt hour. This compares with the national average of about 10 cents per kilowatt hour U.S. consumers now pay for electricity from conventional sources. Dr. Balakirev says, "The state should instead spend the money on energy conservation, wind power, or research into lower-cost ways of harnessing solar power."

---

156. What is the aim of the California program?

    (A) To encourage the use of solar power
    (B) To ease regulations on energy companies
    (C) To open local energy markets to outside suppliers
    (D) To help educate the public about energy conservation

Mark Your Answer:

157. What is the present cost of a kilowatt hour of solar electricity?

    (A) $0.10
    (B) $0.24
    (C) $0.26
    (D) $0.37

Mark Your Answer:

158. What does Sergei Balakirev imply about the California program?

    (A) The money might be better spent in other ways.
    (B) It will help solar power companies expand their production.
    (C) The amount to be spent will not be enough to solve the problem.
    (D) It will encourage businesses to invest more in solar energy technology.

Mark Your Answer:

Practice 2

Questions 159–161 refer to the following graph.

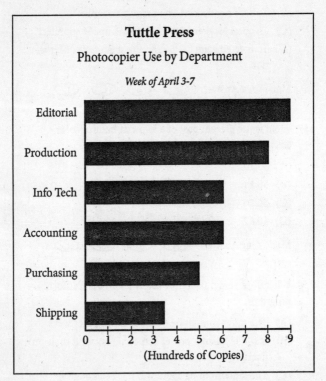

Tuttle Press

Photocopier Use by Department

Week of April 3-7

159. Which department made the most copies during the period shown?

(A) Editorial
(B) Production
(C) Purchasing
(D) Shipping

Mark Your Answer: (A) (B) (C) (D)

160. What was the total number of copies made by the Accounting department during the period shown?

(A) 525
(B) 600
(C) 725
(D) 900

Mark Your Answer: (A) (B) (C) (D)

161. What can be said about the Info Tech department?

(A) Its photocopier usage has increased from previous weeks.
(B) It usually makes fewer photocopies than the Purchasing department.
(C) Its photocopier use equaled the Accounting department's for the week shown.
(D) It made half of all the photocopies at Tuttle Press during the period shown.

Mark Your Answer: (A) (B) (C) (D)

Practice 3

Questions 163–167 refer to the following two letters.

Tipografia Freccia Milano
Via Marconi 1
I-20123 Milan, Italy

10 January 20--

Ms. Suzanne LeBlanc
Tout Pour le Bureau
22, rue du Grenier-Saint-Lazare
75003, Paris, France

Dear Ms. LeBlanc,

Thank you for the catalogs and brochures describing your automatic punching and binding machines. The specifications are certainly very impressive, and we are eager to have our technical people get hands-on experience with their operation, and to examine their build quality and durability.

I understand that your company regularly exhibits at the Macchine di Affari trade fair in Milan. Will you be attending the trade fair next month? If so, would you have the P26, B37, and PB155 models available to demonstrate to our product manager, Mr. Salvatore Accardo?

I look forward to hearing from you.

Sincerely,

Anna Freccia

Director,
Tipografia Freccia Milano

Tout Pour le Bureau
22, rue du Grenier-Saint-Lazare
75003, Paris, France

14 January, 20--

Ms. Anna Freccia
Tipografia Freccia Milano
Via Marconi 1
I-20123 Milan, Italy

Dear Ms. Freccia,

Thank you for your letter of January 10th and for your interest in our products. I am pleased to inform you that we will indeed be exhibiting in Milan next month and will be delighted to demonstrate the P26, B37, and PB155 to Mr. Accardo. We will be exhibiting on all three days and are normally quite busy, due to the lively interest in our office machines. I suggest that Mr. Accardo schedule a meeting with our sales manager, Mr. Didier Lafontaine, to ensure that he is able to get a full demonstration of our products and ask any questions he may have. Please let me know if you would like to arrange a time for this.

In the meantime, I am enclosing copies of several endorsements from satisfied customers in Italy. They have indicated that you are welcome to contact them concerning our company and our products.

I look forward to your response.

Sincerely,

Suzanne LeBlanc
Head of Sales and Marketing,
Tout Pour le Bureau

163. What does Tipografia Freccia want to learn regarding Tout Pour le Bureau's machines?

    (A) How well they operate
    (B) The cost to ship them to Italy
    (C) How quickly they can be delivered
    (D) The amount of operator training required

    Mark Your Answer:

164. Who is Mr. Accardo?

    (A) A salesperson
    (B) A product manager
    (C) One of Tipografia Freccia's best customers
    (D) The head of Tipografia Freccia's Paris branch

    Mark Your Answer:

165. What is learned about the Macchine di Affari trade fair in Milan?

    (A) It lasts for three days.
    (B) It is held every October.
    (C) It is held only every other year.
    (D) It is the largest trade fair in Italy.

    Mark Your Answer:

166. What does Ms. LeBlanc suggest that Mr. Accardo do?

    (A) Visit her company's factory

    (B) Arrive at the exhibit hall early

    (C) Arrange to meet with a sales manger

    (D) Get shipping quotes from several companies

    Mark Your Answer:

167. The word "endorsements" in paragraph 2 line 1 is closest in meaning to

    (A) invoices

    (B) signatures

    (C) authorizations

    (D) recommendations

    Mark Your Answer:

ANSWERS AND EXPLANATIONS

Practice 1

Questions 156–158 refer to the following article.

State Approves $2.5 billion Solar Subsidy

California regulators have approved a $2.5 billion subsidy package for solar power. The subsidy program is the largest ever in the United States and promises more business for solar panel manufacturers such as SunTastic and SolarWatt who are already struggling to meet current levels of demand.

The state plans to hand out the money over the next 10 years in the form of rebates for consumers and businesses that install solar power facilities. It will probably be several years before manufacturers can meet rising demand for solar panels. Producers in Germany and other European countries also have backlogs of orders.

Global production of solar panels grew 37 percent last year, according to figures provided by the consulting firm Solar Tech Research, and manufacturers everywhere are selling all they can produce. Supporters of the California subsidy say it will encourage manufacturers to add the necessary capacity to meet the demand. Opponents suggest that the move may only serve to keep prices high.

Dr. Sergei Balakirev, director of the Energy Institute at the California Technical College, says that the price of solar power is still too high, which discourages most people from adopting the technology. A typical residential system costs $24,000 to install and yields electricity costing about 26 cents per kilowatt hour. This compares with the national average of about 10 cents per kilowatt hour U.S. consumers now pay for electricity from conventional sources. Dr. Balakirev says, "The state should instead spend the money on energy conservation, wind power, or research into lower-cost ways of harnessing solar power."

---

156. What is the aim of the California program?

    (A) To encourage the use of solar power
    (B) To ease regulations on energy companies
    (C) To open local energy markets to outside suppliers
    (D) To help educate the public about energy conservation

Explanation: This is a Gist question. The correct answer is Choice (A).

Choice (B) uses the passage word *regulations* and uses an idea related to the passage content, but it is incorrect. This is an "incorrect paraphrase/misstatement" distractor.

Choices (C) and (D) are "not mentioned" distractors.

157. What is the present cost of a kilowatt hour of solar electricity?

    (A) $0.10
    (B) $0.24
    (C) $0.26
    (D) $0.37

Explanation: This is a Detail question. The correct answer is Choice (C).

Choice (A) is mentioned in the passage, but it is wrong. This is a "repeated words" distractor. Choice (B) is based on misreading *$24,000*. This is an "incorrect paraphrase/misstatement" distractor. Choice (D) is based on misreading *37 percent*. This is a "repeated words" distractor.

158. What does Sergei Balakirev imply about the California program?

(A) The money might be better spent in other ways.

(B) It will help solar power companies expand their production.

(C) The amount to be spent will not be enough to solve the problem.

(D) It will encourage businesses to invest more in solar energy technology.

Explanation: This is an Inference/Implication question. The correct answer is Choice (A).

Choices (B), (C), and (D) are "not mentioned" distractors.

Practice 2

Questions 159–161 refer to the following graph.

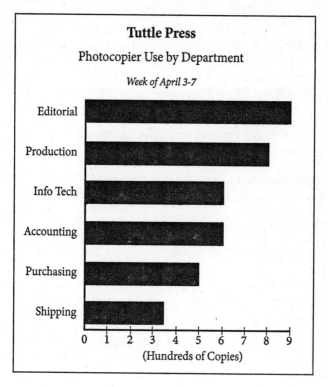

159. Which department made the most copies during the period shown?

   (A) Editorial
   (B) Production
   (C) Purchasing
   (D) Shipping

Explanation: This is a Detail question. The correct answer is Choice (A).

Choices (B), (C), and (D) are all found in the passage but are wrong. These are "repeated words" distractors.

160. What was the total number of copies made by the Accounting department during the period shown?

   (A) 525
   (B) 600
   (C) 725
   (D) 900

Explanation: This is a Detail question. The correct answer is Choice (B).

Choices (A), (C), and (D) are all found in the passage, but they are wrong. These are "repeated words" distractors.

161. What can be said about the Info Tech department?

    (A) Its photocopier usage has increased from previous weeks.

    (B) It usually makes fewer photocopies than the Purchasing department.

    (C) Its photocopier use equaled the Accounting department's for the week shown.

    (D) It made half of all the photocopies at Tuttle Press during the period shown.

Explanation: This is an Inference/Implication question. The correct answer is Choice (C).

Because choices (A) and (B) cannot be determined from the graph, they are "not mentioned" distractors.

Choice (D) is not true. It is an "incorrect paraphrase/misstatement" distractor.

Practice 3

Questions 163–167 refer to the following two letters.

Tipografia Freccia Milano
Via Marconi 1
I-20123 Milan, Italy

10 January 20--

Ms. Suzanne LeBlanc
Tout Pour le Bureau
22, rue du Grenier-Saint-Lazare
75003, Paris, France

Dear Ms. LeBlanc,

Thank you for the catalogs and brochures describing your automatic punching and binding machines. The specifications are certainly very impressive, and we are eager to have our technical people get hands-on experience with their operation, and to examine their build quality and durability.

I understand that your company regularly exhibits at the Macchine di Affari trade fair in Milan. Will you be attending the trade fair next month? If so, would you have the P26, B37, and PB155 models available to demonstrate to our product manager, Mr. Salvatore Accardo?

I look forward to hearing from you.

Sincerely,

Anna Freccia

Director,
Tipografia Freccia Milano

Tout Pour le Bureau
22, rue du Grenier-Saint-Lazare
75003, Paris, France

14 January, 20--

Ms. Anna Freccia
Tipografia Freccia Milano
Via Marconi 1
I-20123 Milan, Italy

Dear Ms. Freccia,

Thank you for your letter of January 10th and for your interest in our products. I am pleased to inform you that we will indeed be exhibiting in Milan next month and will be delighted to demonstrate the P26, B37, and PB155 to Mr. Accardo. We will be exhibiting on all three days and are normally quite busy, due to the lively interest in our office machines. I suggest that Mr. Accardo schedule a meeting with our sales manager, Mr. Didier Lafontaine, to ensure that he is able to get a full demonstration of our products and ask any questions he may have. Please let me know if you would like to arrange a time for this.

In the meantime, I am enclosing copies of several endorsements from satisfied customers in Italy. They have indicated that you are welcome to contact them concerning our company and our products.

I look forward to your response.

Sincerely,

Suzanne LeBlanc
Head of Sales and Marketing,
Tout Pour le Bureau

163. What does Tipografia Freccia want to learn regarding Tout Pour le Bureau's machines?

(A) How well they operate

(B) The cost to ship them to Italy

(C) How quickly they can be delivered

(D) The amount of operator training required

Explanation: This is a Detail question. The correct answer is Choice (A).

Choices (B) and (C) are "not mentioned" distractors. Choice (D) plays on the passage word *operation,* but as a whole it is a "not mentioned" distractor.

164. Who is Mr. Accardo?

(A) A salesperson

(B) A product manager

(C) One of Tipografia Freccia's best customers

(D) The head of Tipografia Freccia's Paris branch

Explanation: This is a Detail question. The correct answer is Choice (B).

Choices (A), (C), and (D) are not mentioned distractors.

165. What is learned about the Macchine di Affari trade fair in Milan?

(A) It lasts for three days.

(B) It is held every October.

(C) It is held only every other year.

(D) It is the largest trade fair in Italy.

Explanation: This is an Inference/Implication question. The correct answer is Choice (A). Ms. LeBlanc says her company will be attending the trade fair and "exhibiting on all three days."

Choices (A), (C), and (D) are "not mentioned" distractors.

166. What does Ms. LeBlanc suggest that Mr. Accardo do?

   (A) Visit her company's factory
   (B) Arrive at the exhibit hall early
   (C) Arrange to meet with a sales manger
   (D) Get shipping quotes from several companies

Explanation: This is a Detail question. The correct answer is Choice (C).

Choices (A), (B), and (D) are all "not mentioned" distractors.

167. The word "endorsements" in paragraph X line Y is closest in meaning to

   (A) invoices
   (B) signatures
   (C) authorizations
   (D) recommendations

Explanation: This is a Vocabulary question. The correct answer is Choice (D).

Choices (A), (B), and (C) are all incorrect. Distractors for vocabulary questions can be considered "incorrect paraphrase/misstatement." They incorrectly paraphrase the vocabulary word being tested.